*Peggy Louise Parrish*
*Parma, Idaho 83660*

*All interior and cover art by Peggy Louise Parrish*

*ISBN-13: 978-1543294903*
*ISBN-10:1543294901*
*Printed in The United States of America*

The wonderful Letter W is here for you to color in however you will. Some of the W letters in this book have colored examples to visit. Peggy Louise Parrish is the artist that has designed these W Letters. If you want to make a few "in house" copies to color in several ways go ahead. The artist wants you to leave her initials on the bottom and not sell anything you color in this book. Feel free however to make a copy of your colored letters for yourself or a gift.

It can be quite a fun art adventure to color these letter designs, print them onto card stock, add glitter, embellishments and then add the letter to a card for someone. Perhaps your first or last name begins with a W. Maybe you need a decorative W for something you are making for someone. Quality colored pencils are the preferred choice for these letter books. If you want to use markers, watercolor pencils, paints or gel pens try placing a scrap paper behind the page you are coloring on. Then let it dry before moving on.

The other alphabet letters also have their own book if you enjoy this coloring book. Perhaps you will get caught up in letter W so much you will design some of your own. Color till your heart's content.

The Wonderful letter W can be surrounded with a wallpaper effect and filled with plants if you like.

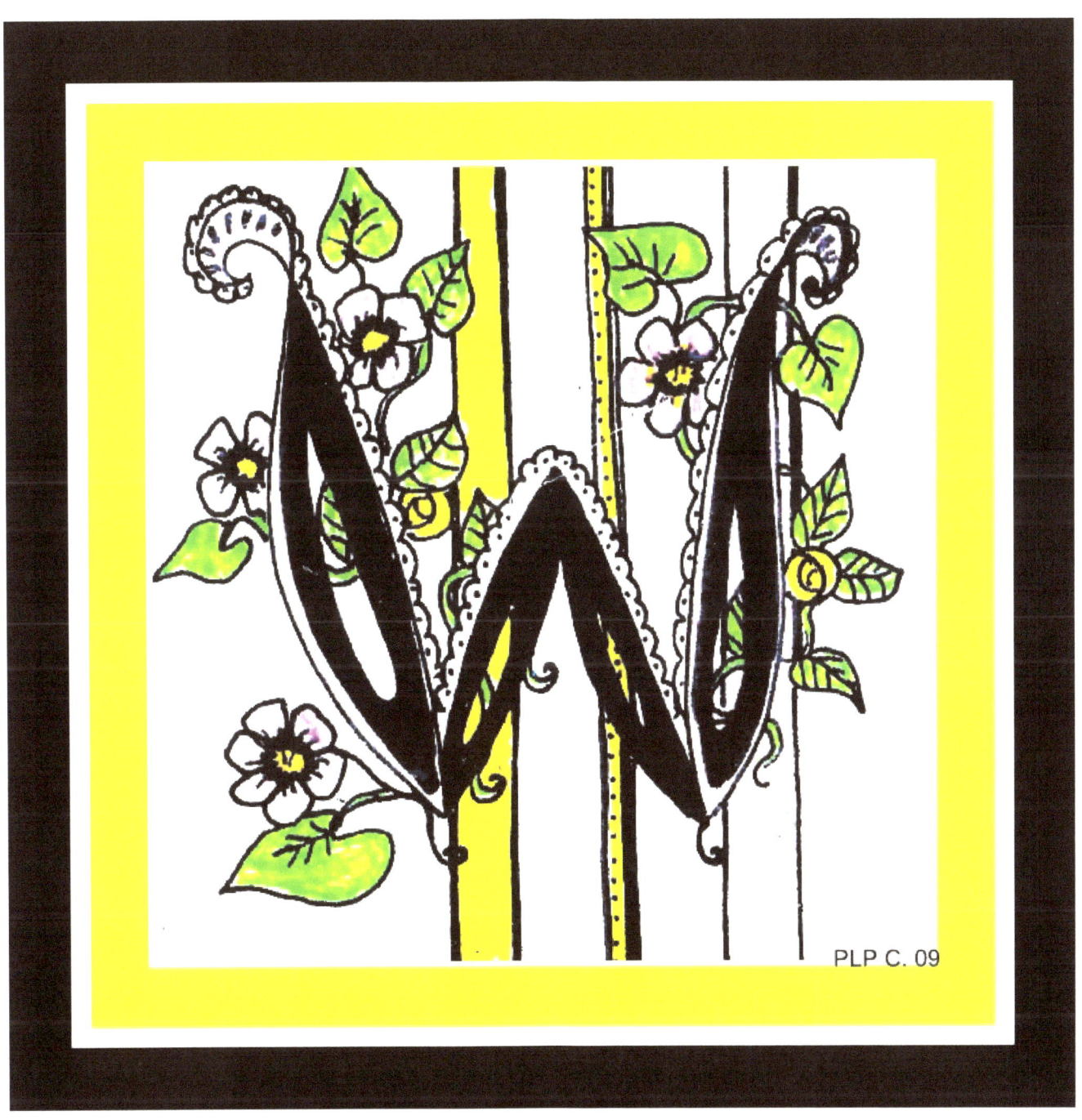

PLP C. 09

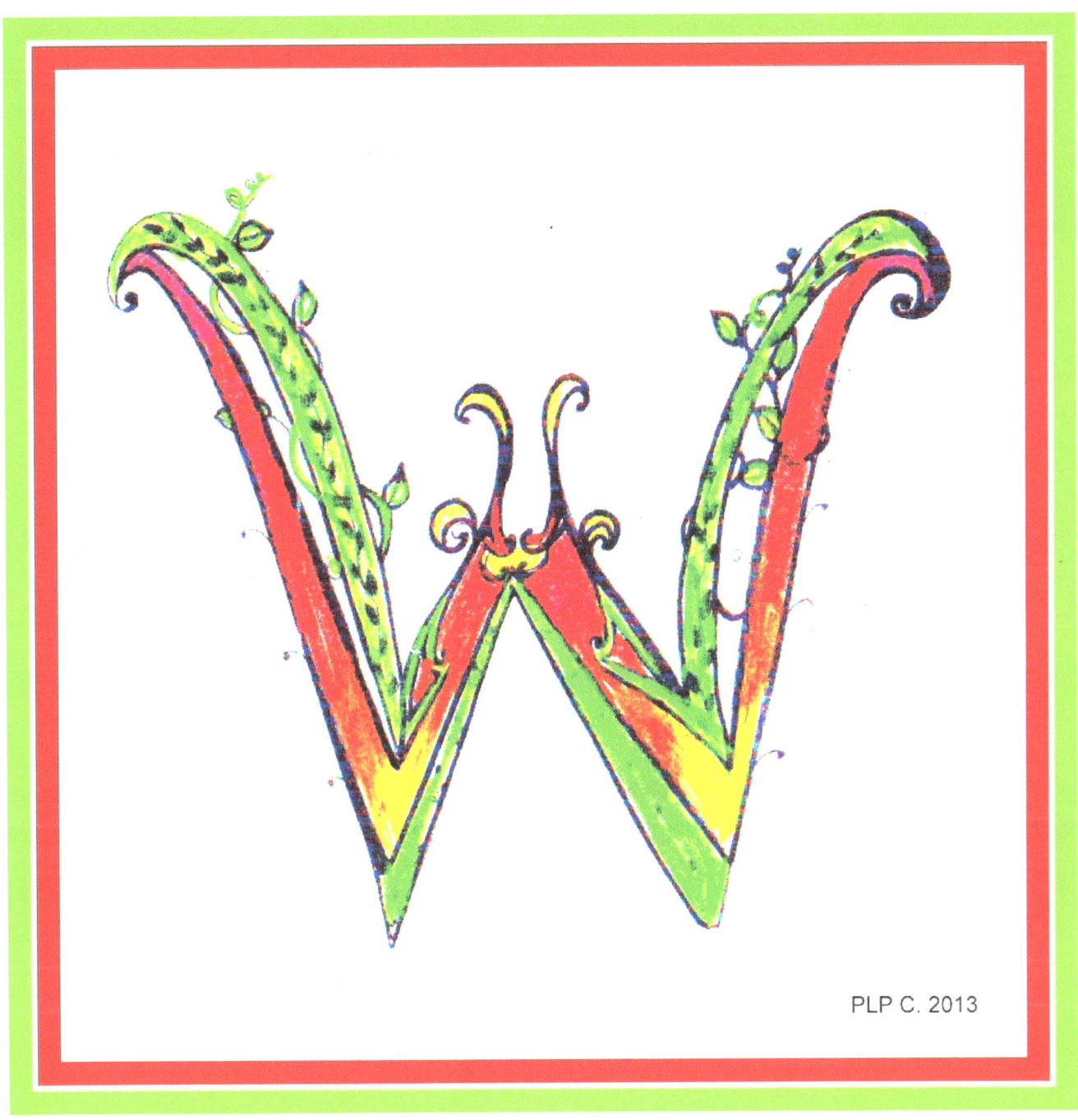

PLP C. 2013

Or the Wonderful W can be beautiful all by itself!

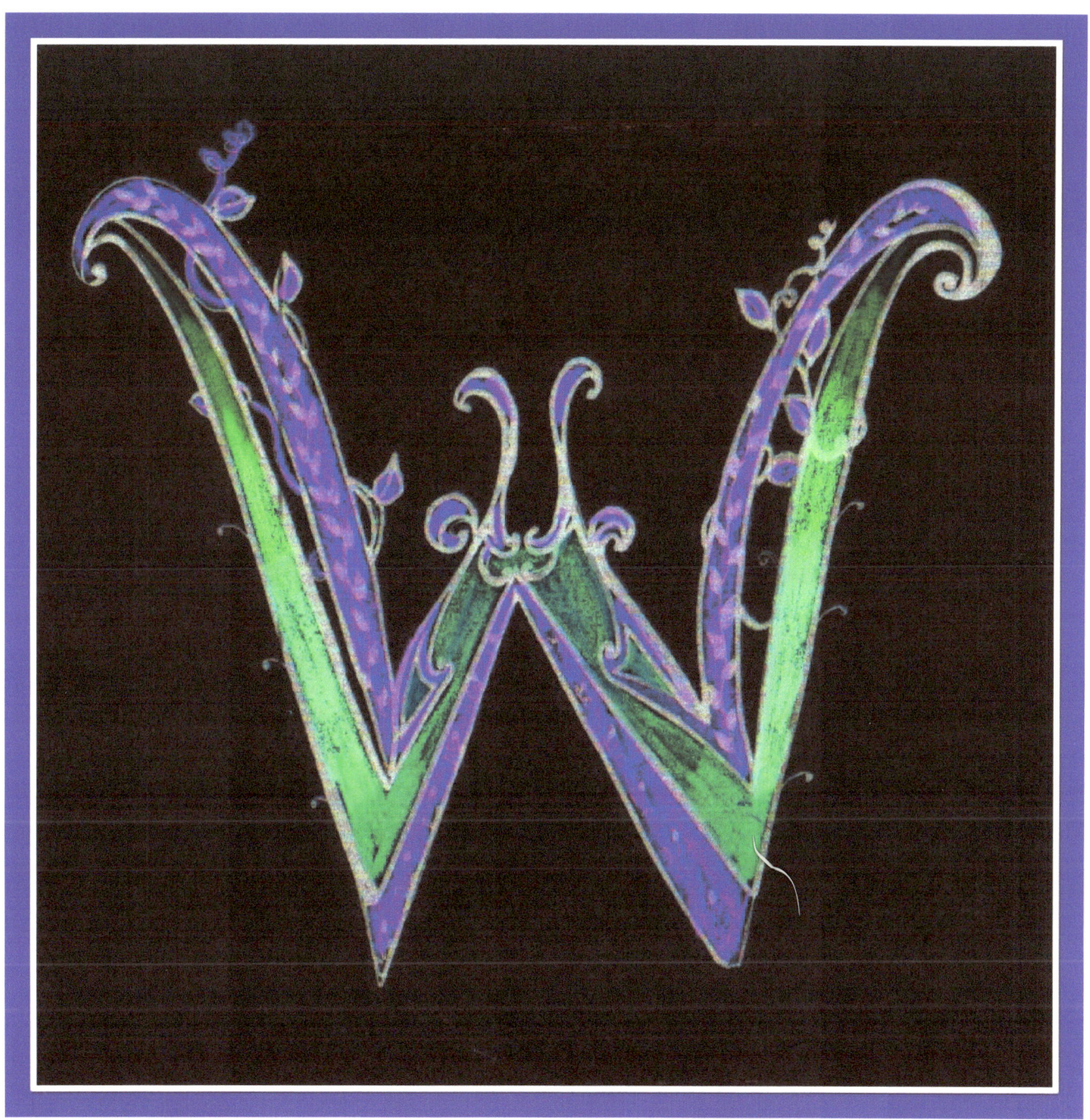

If these colors are inverted on the computer the W

has the opposite colors on the color wheel like this.

Now for some W fun!

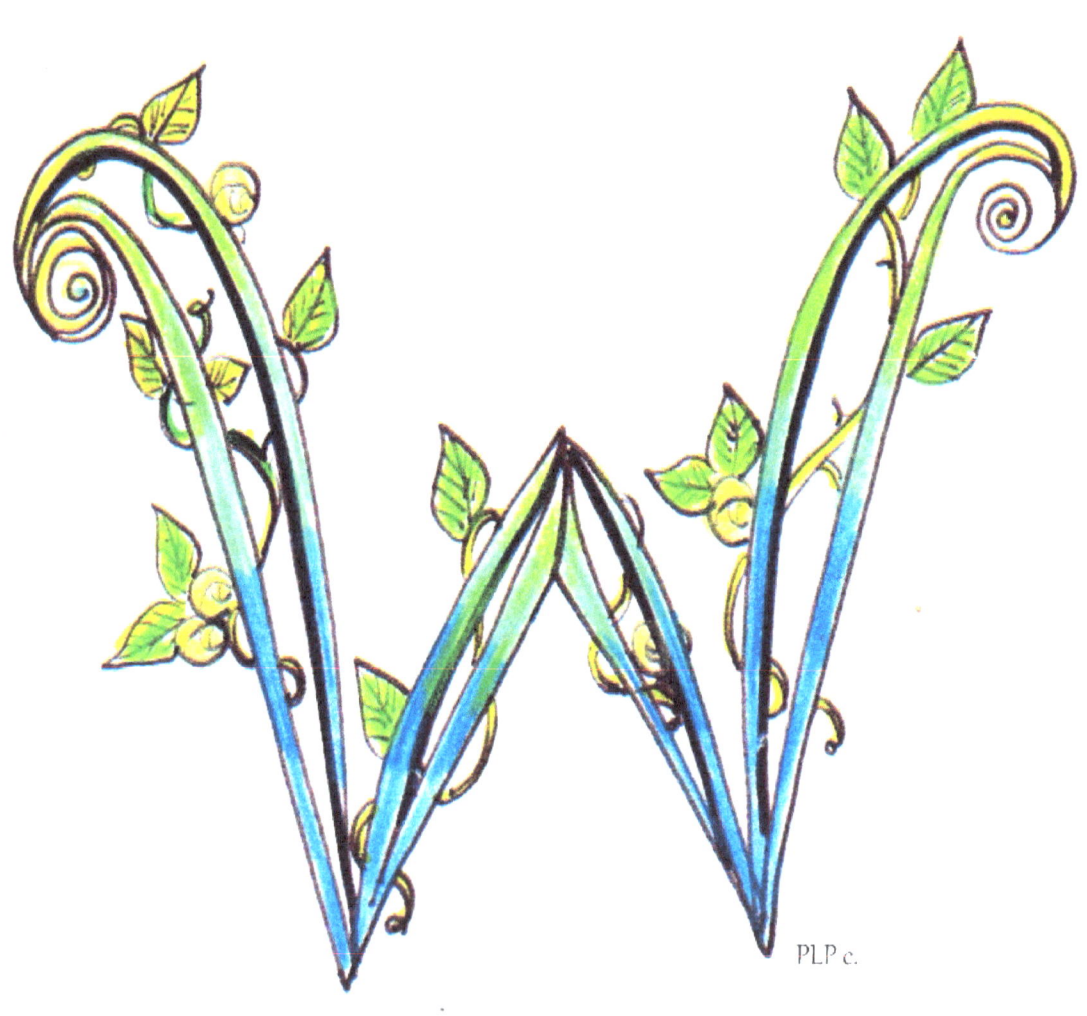

PLP c.

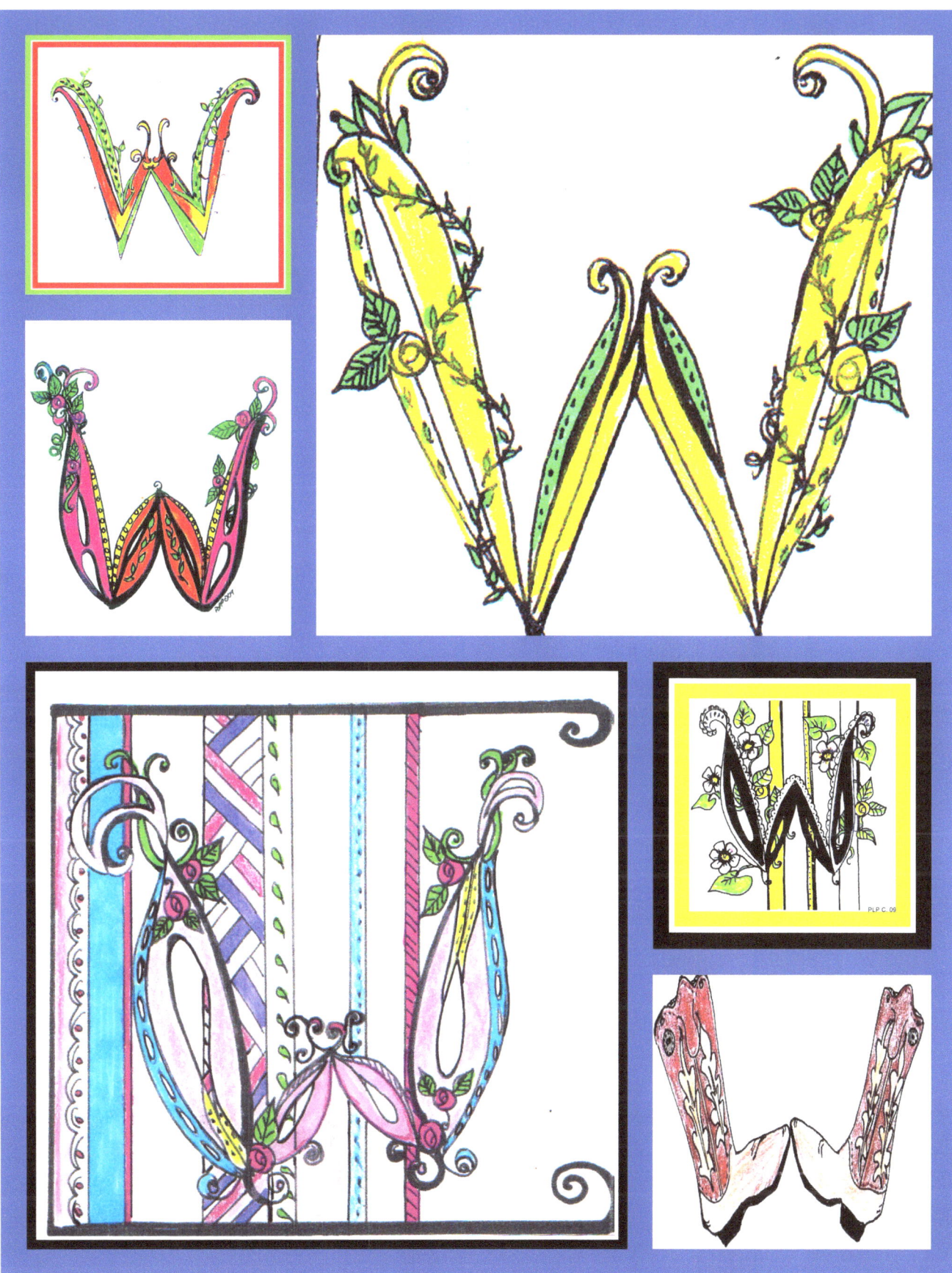

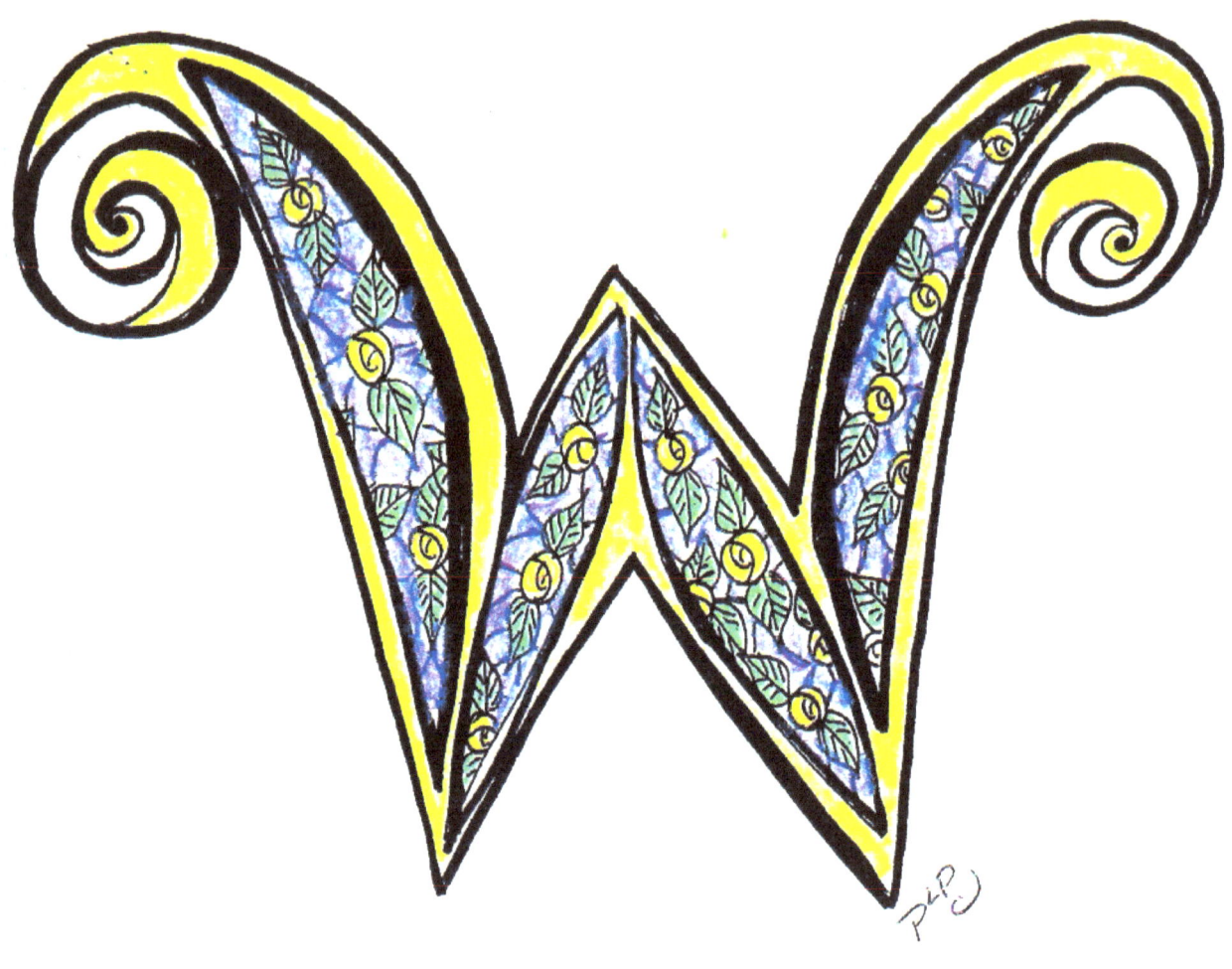

# The Wonderful Letter W

# Coloring Book

By Peggy Louise Parrish
C. 2017

# The Wonderful W

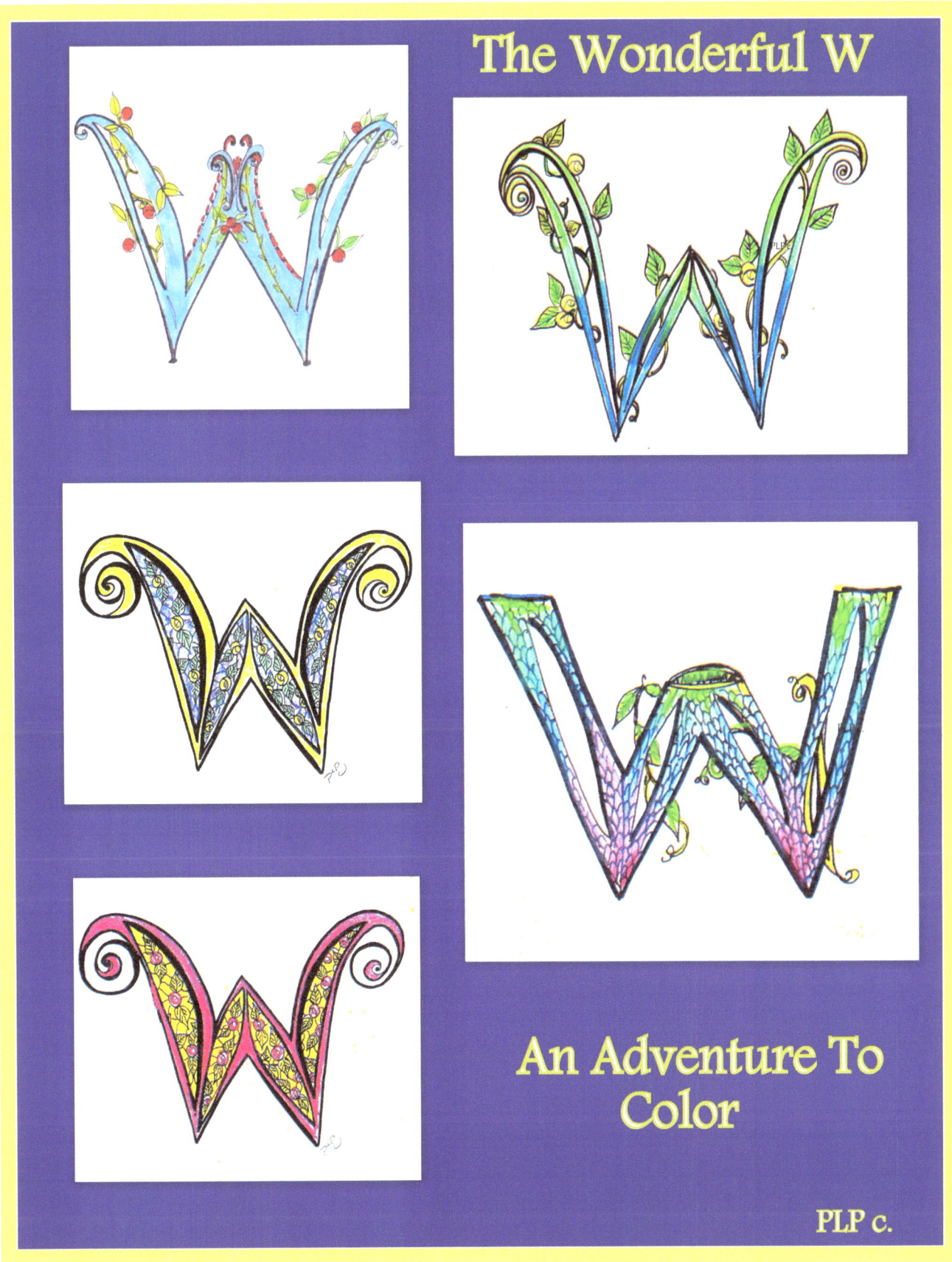

## An Adventure To Color

Wonderful W can go Cowboy . Or it can dress up all sorts of ways.

# Welcome To Wonderful W

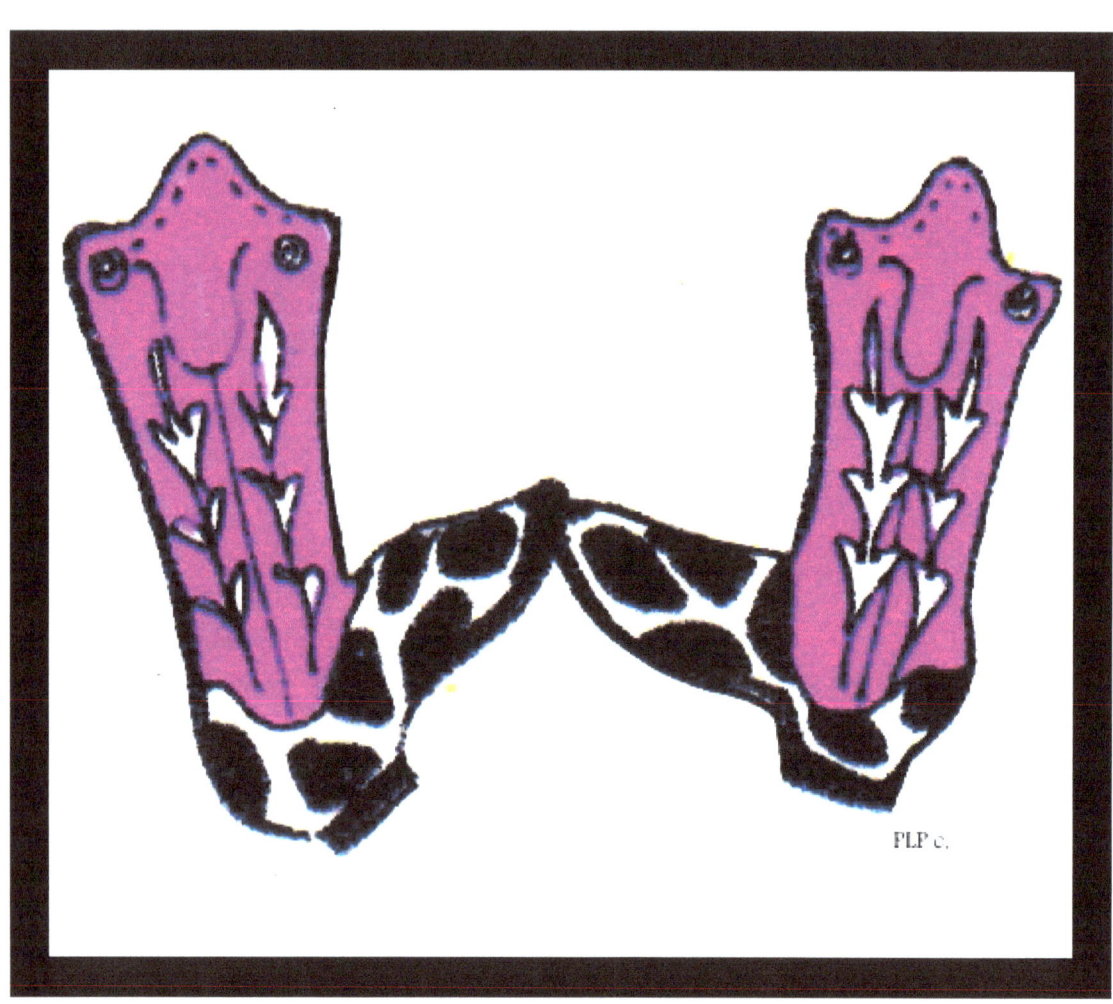

Get your colors ready, get set.....GO

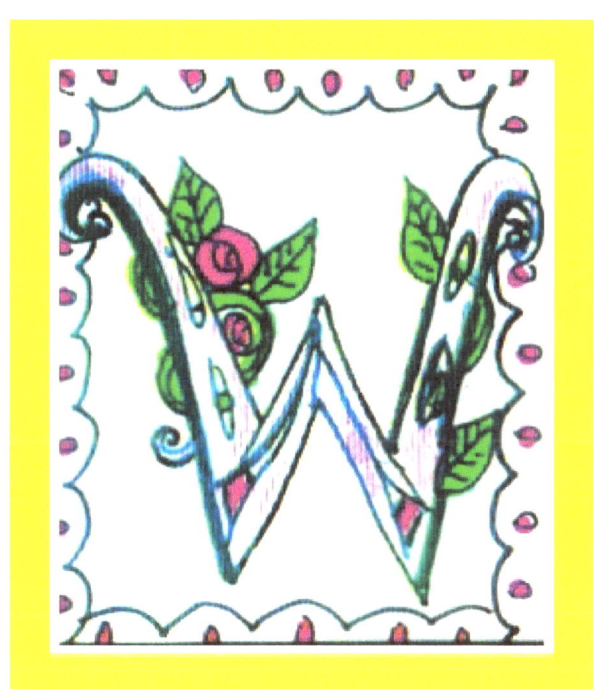

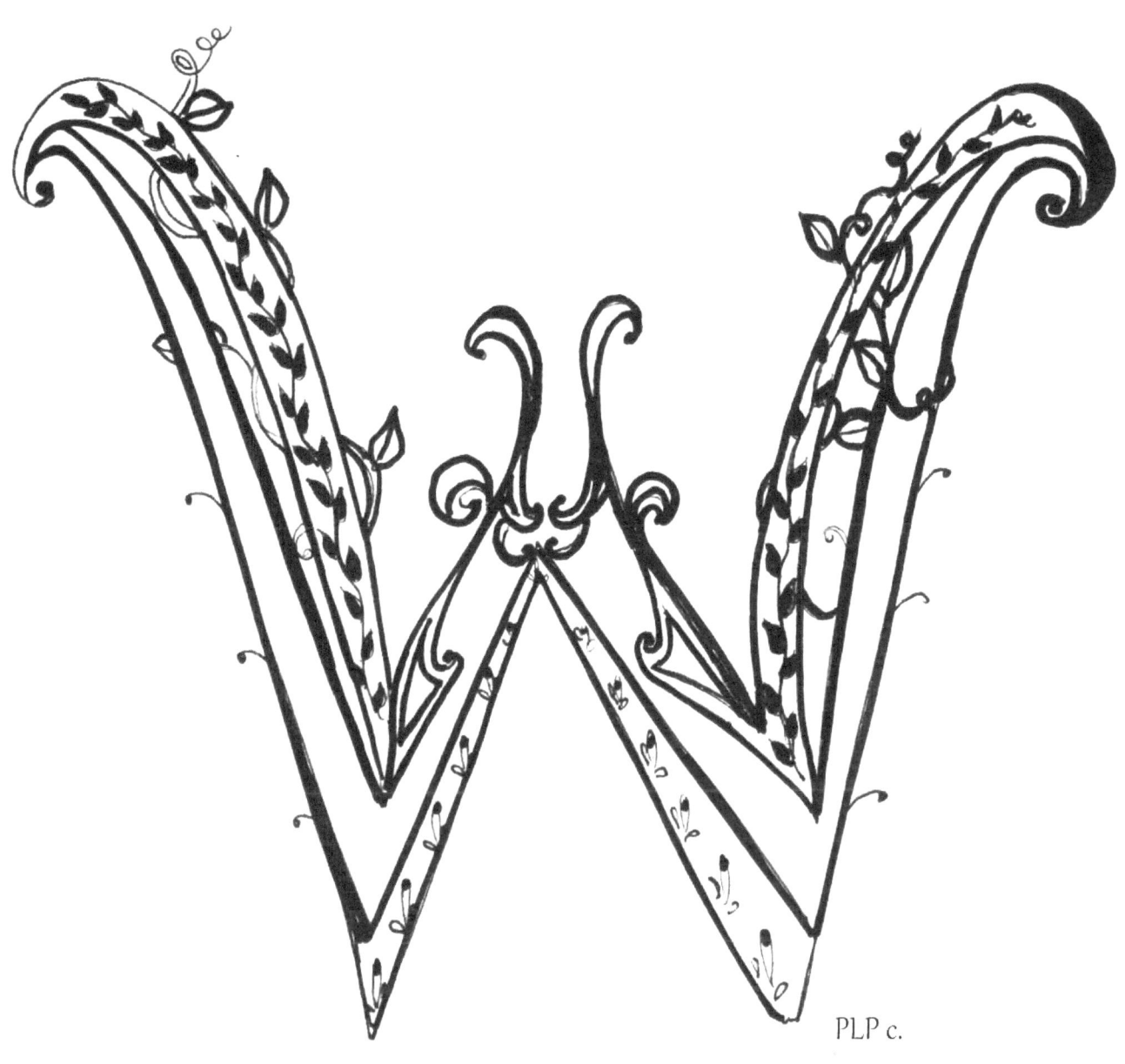

PLP c.

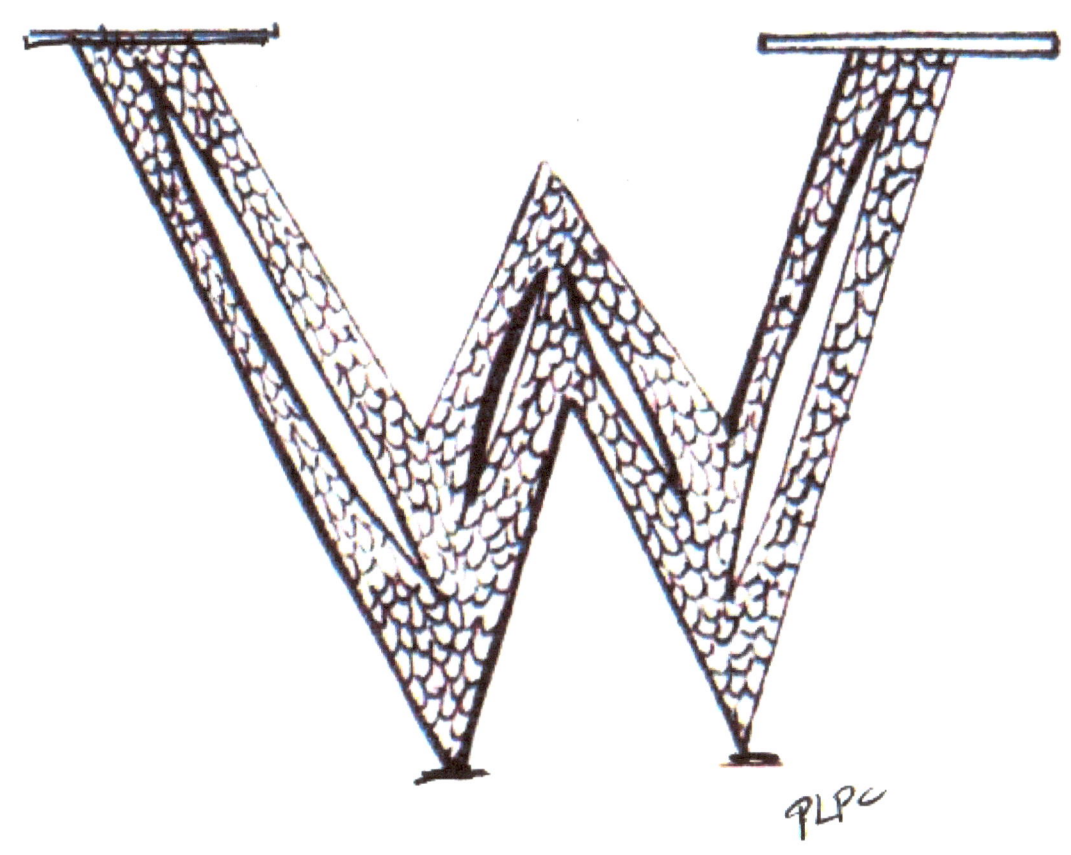

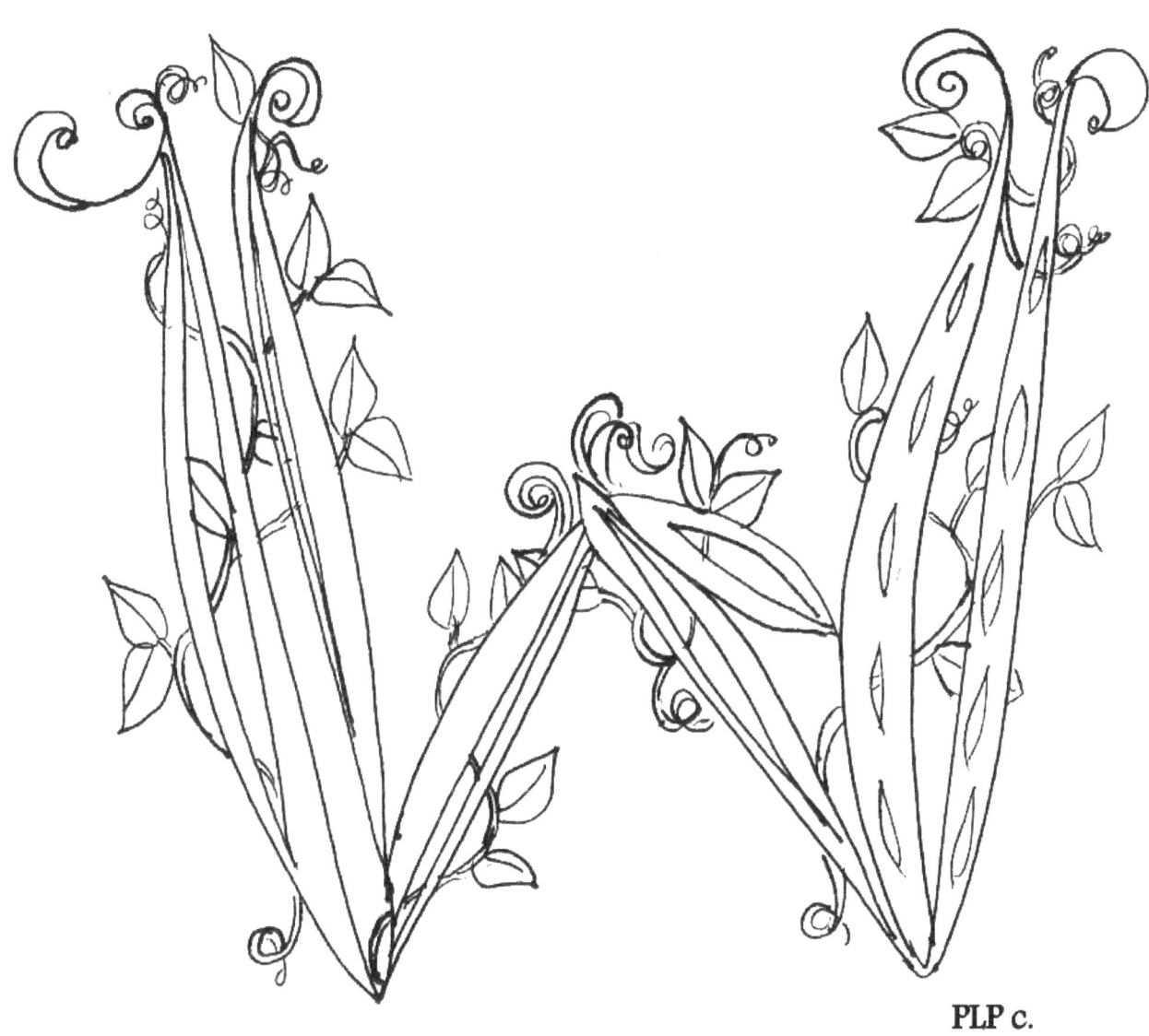

PLP c.

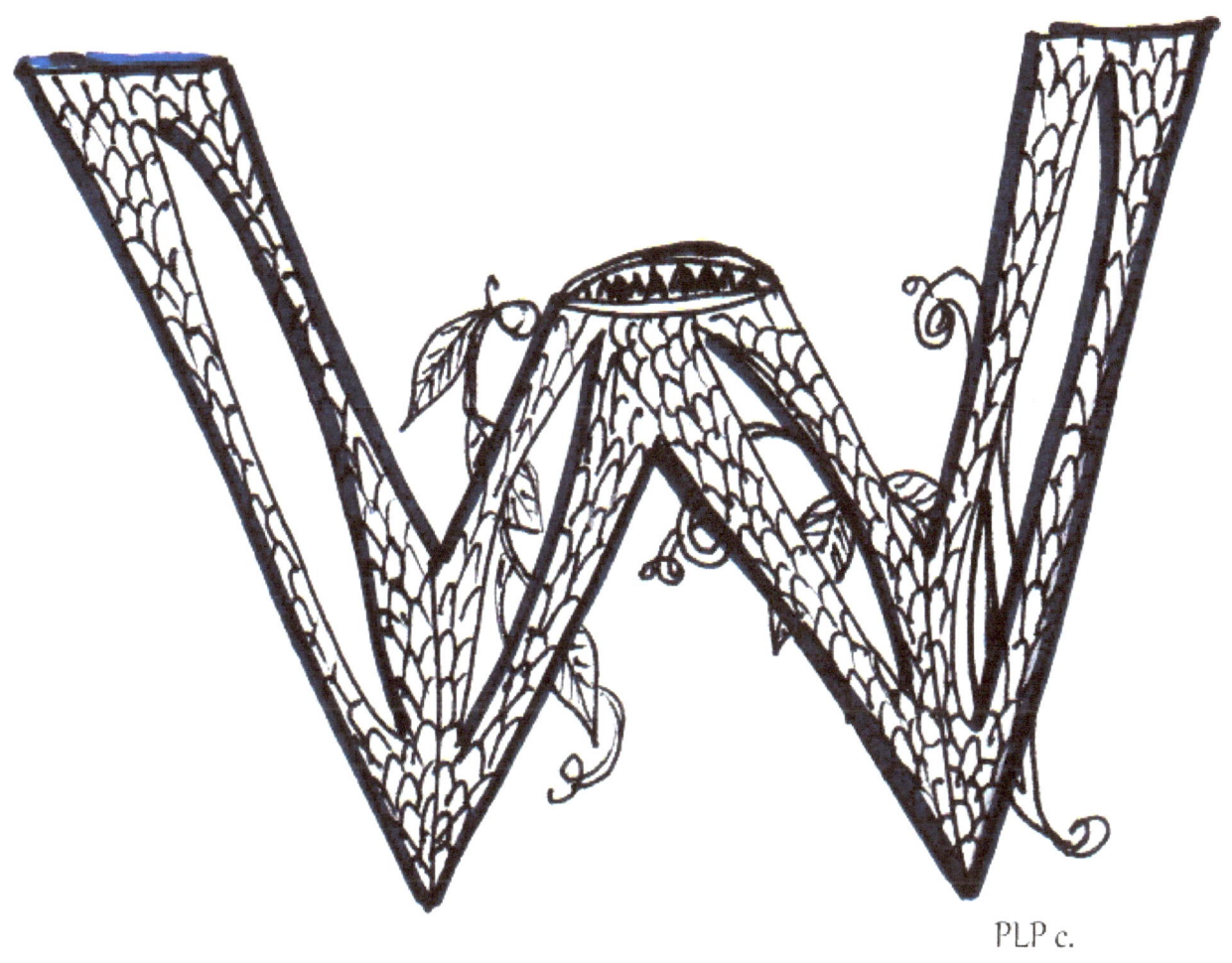

PLP c.

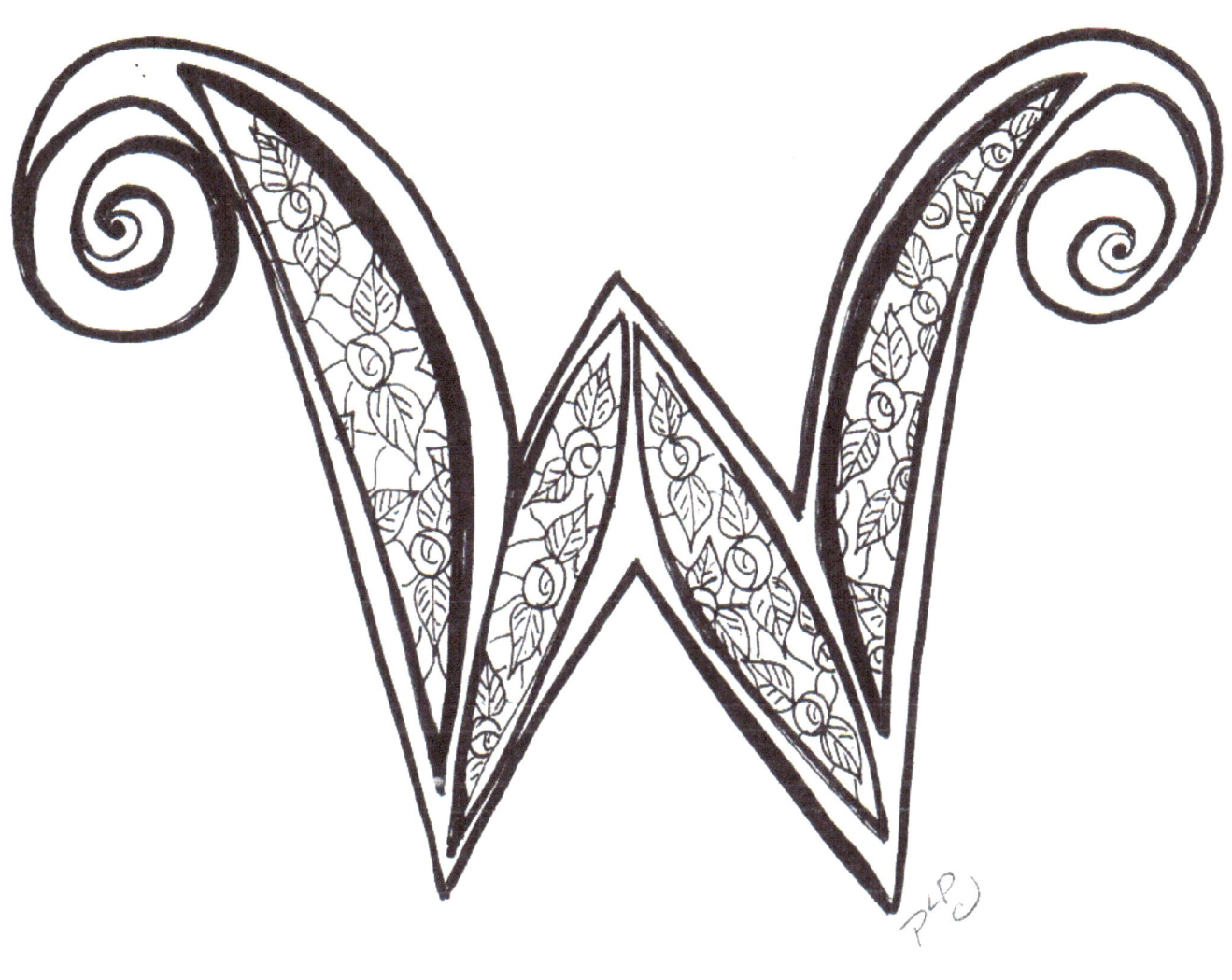

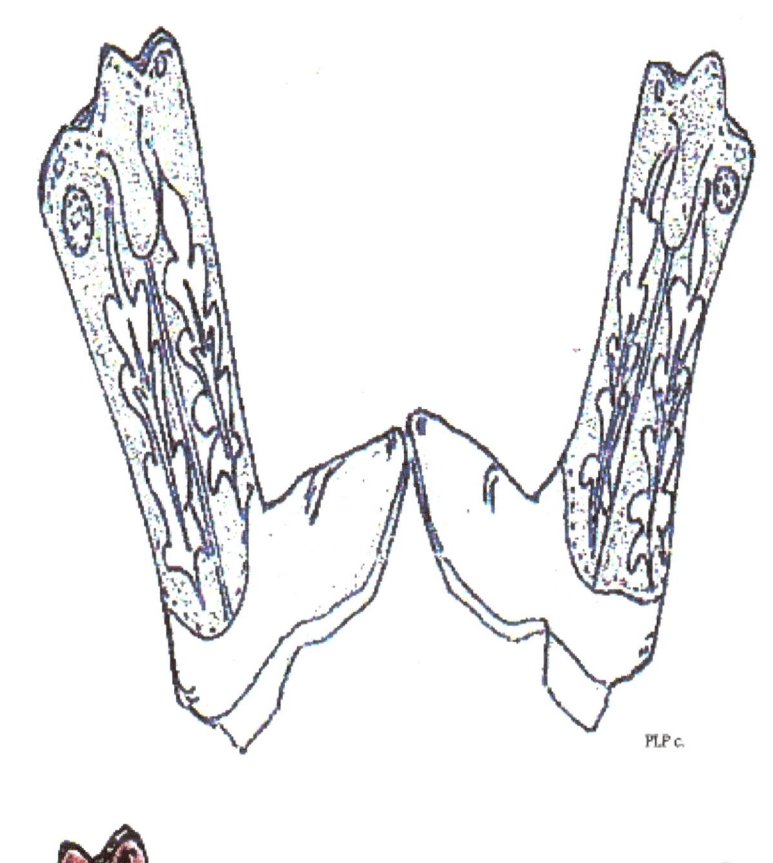

PLP c.

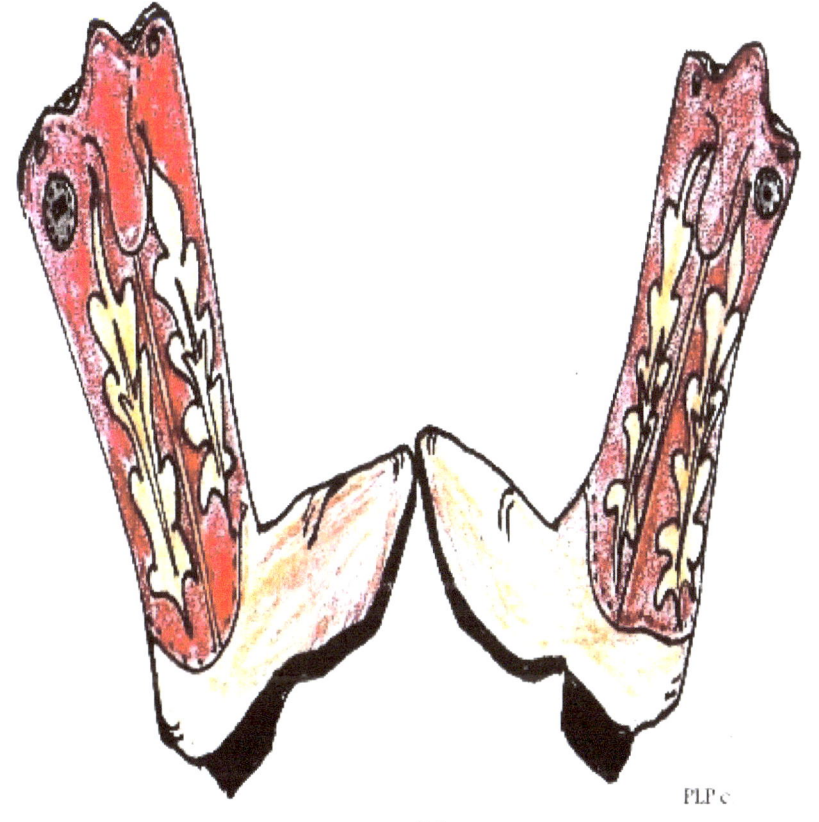

PLP c

29

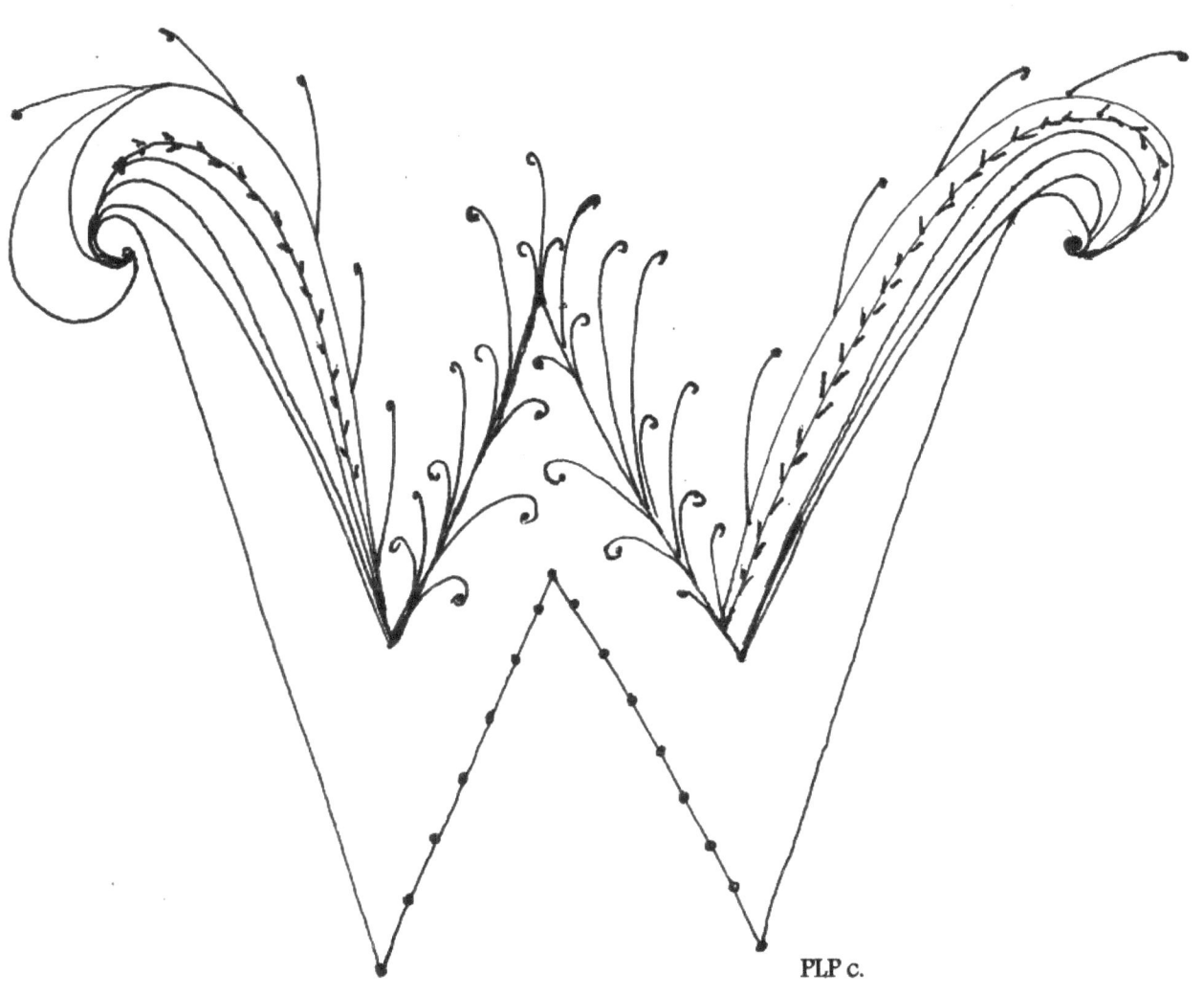

PLP c.

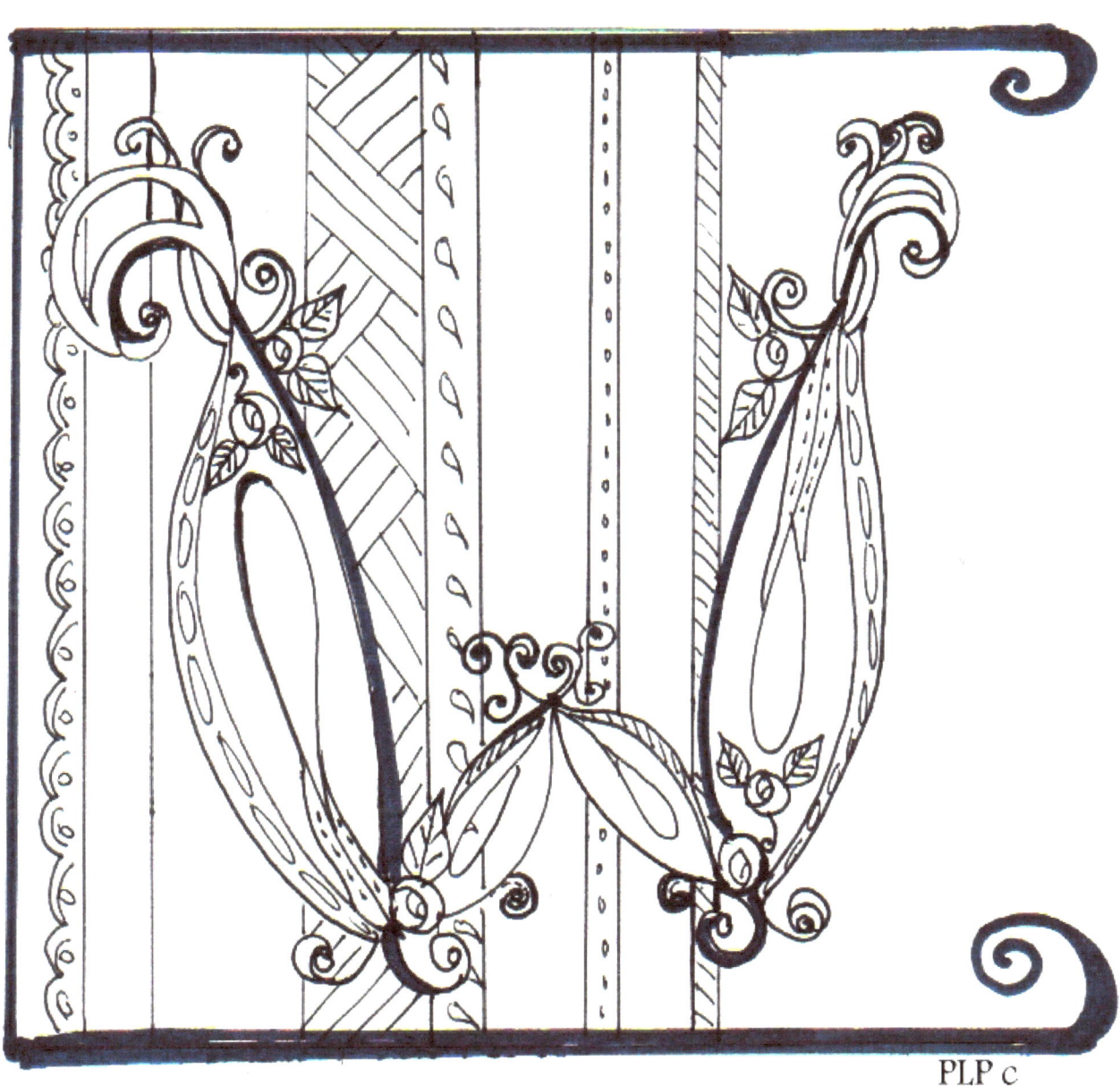

PLP c

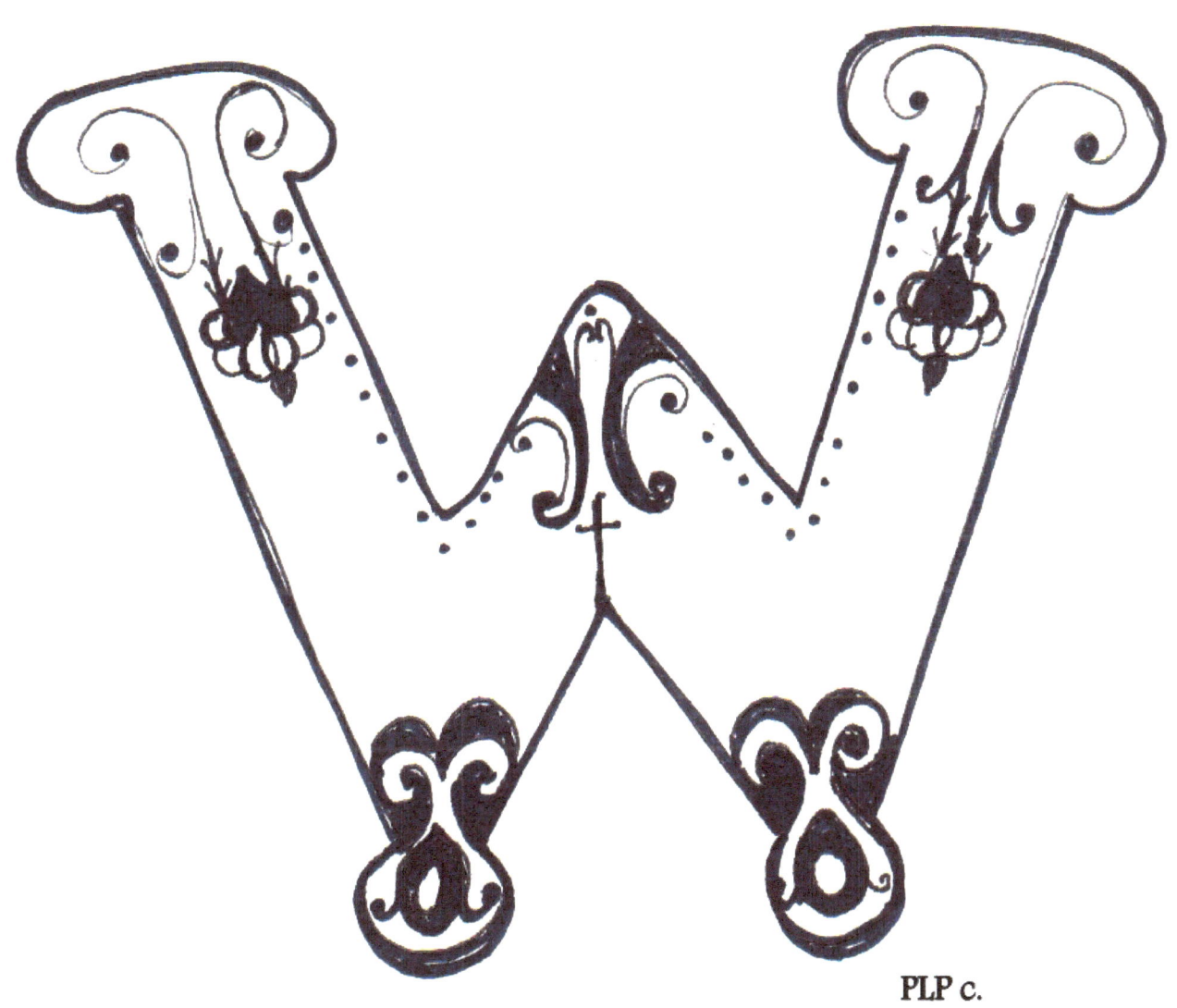

PLP c.

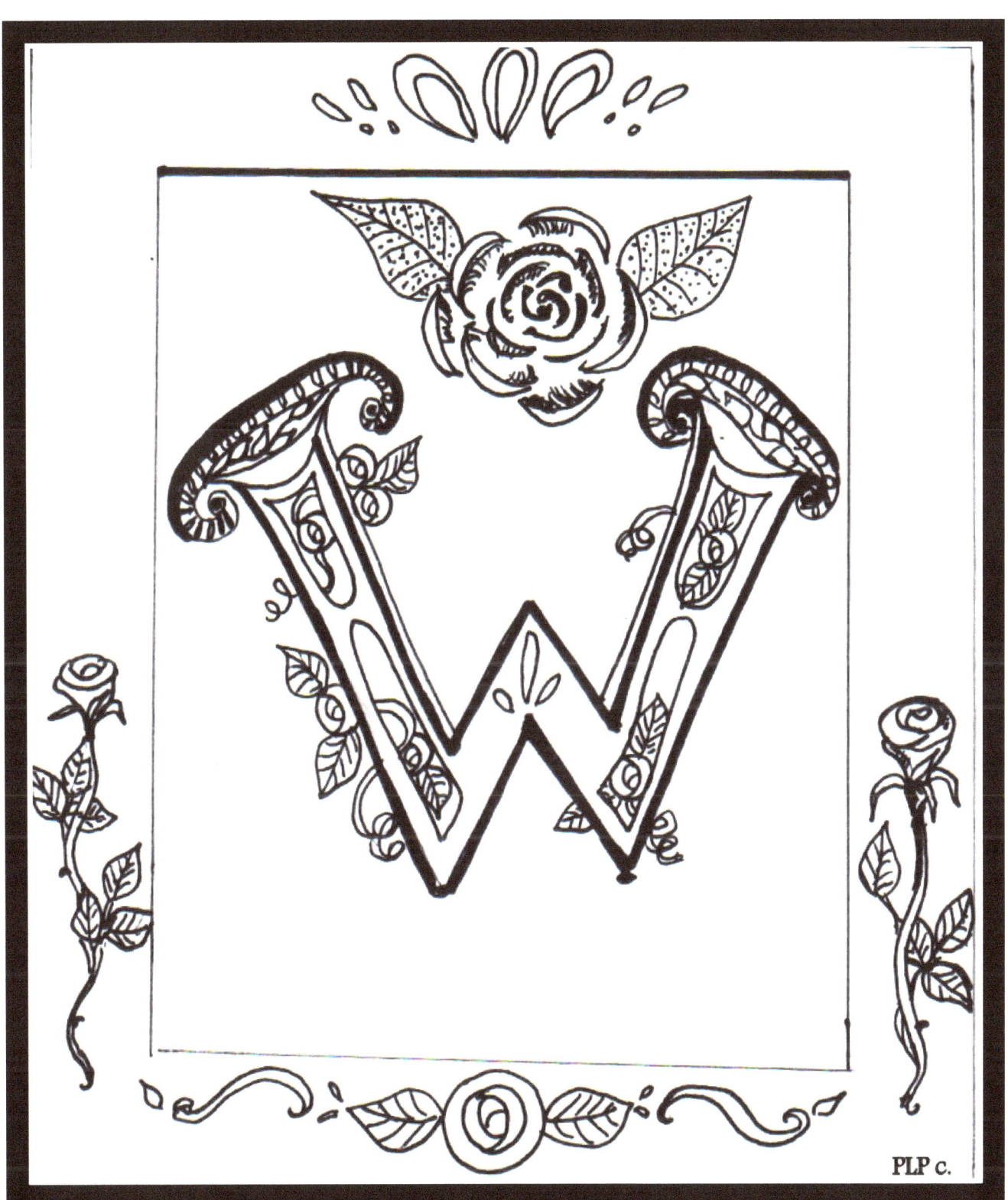

PLP c.

PLP c.

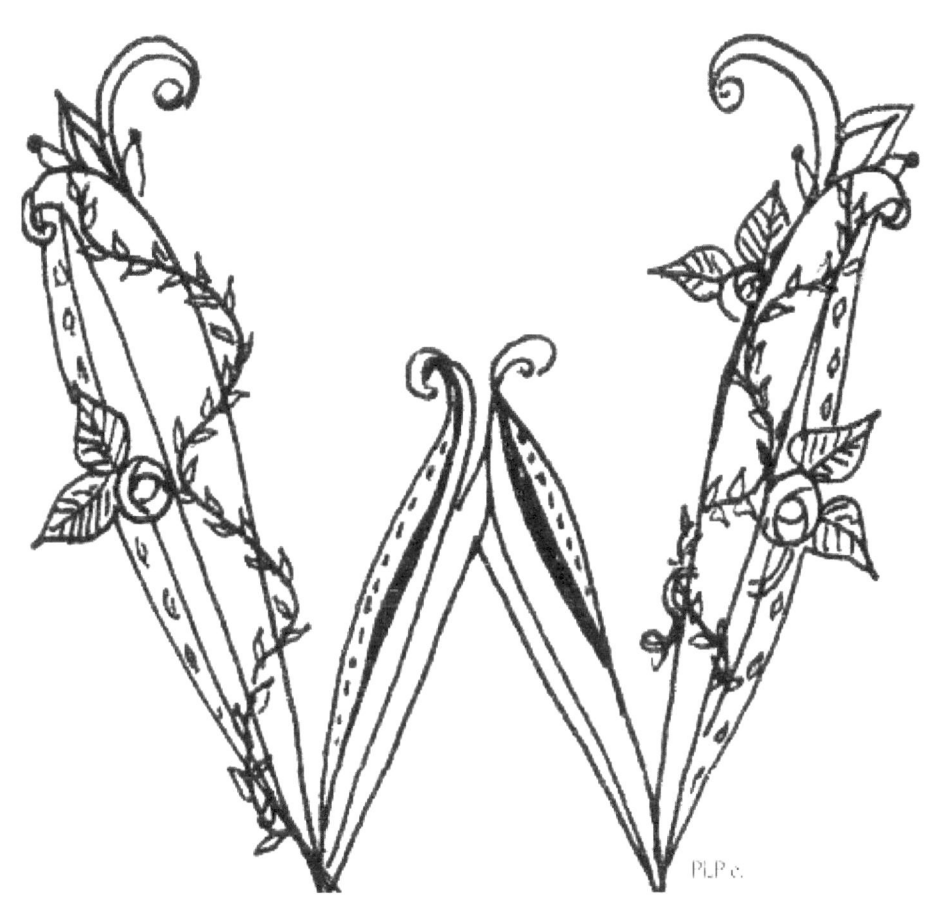

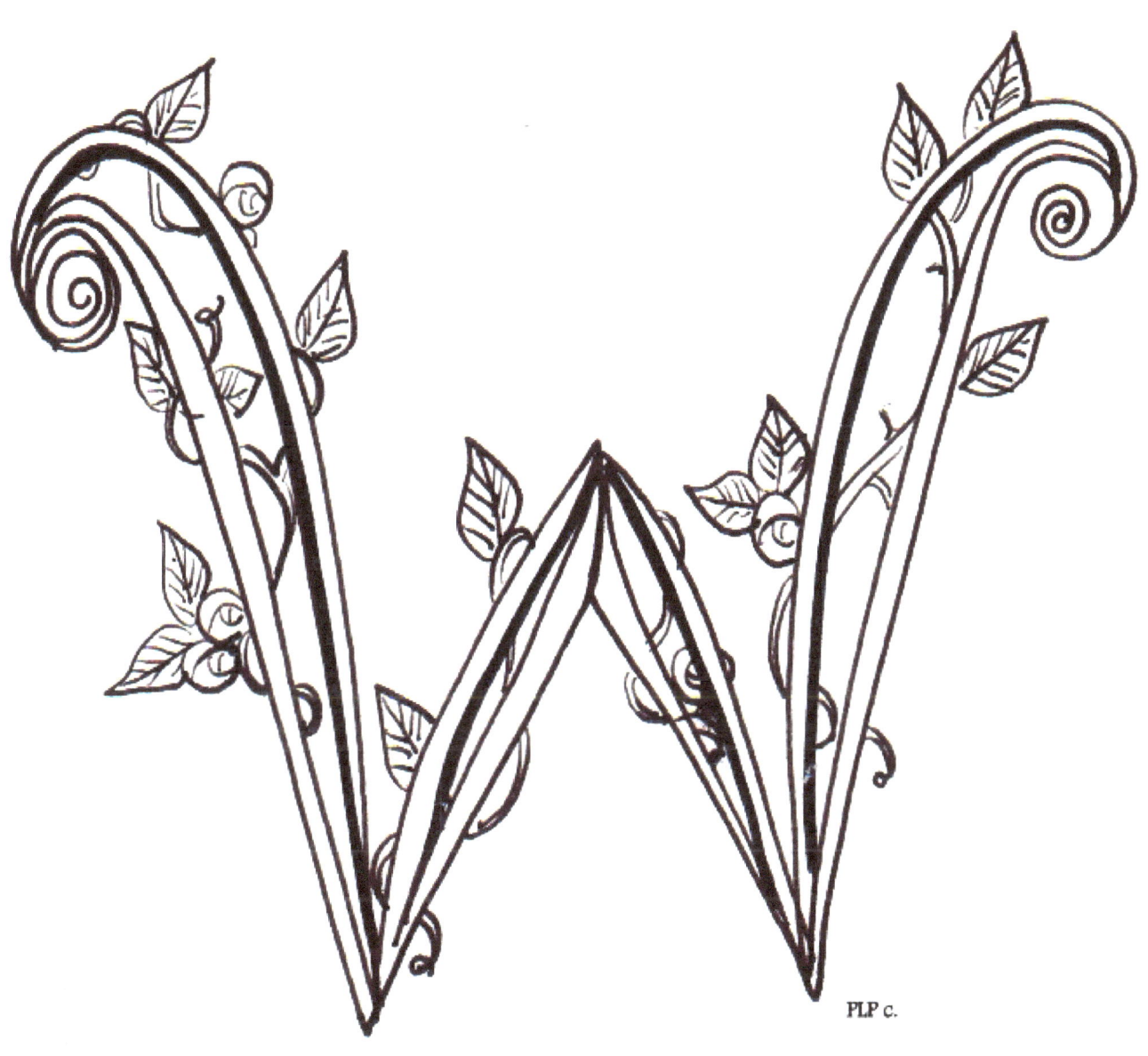

PLF c.

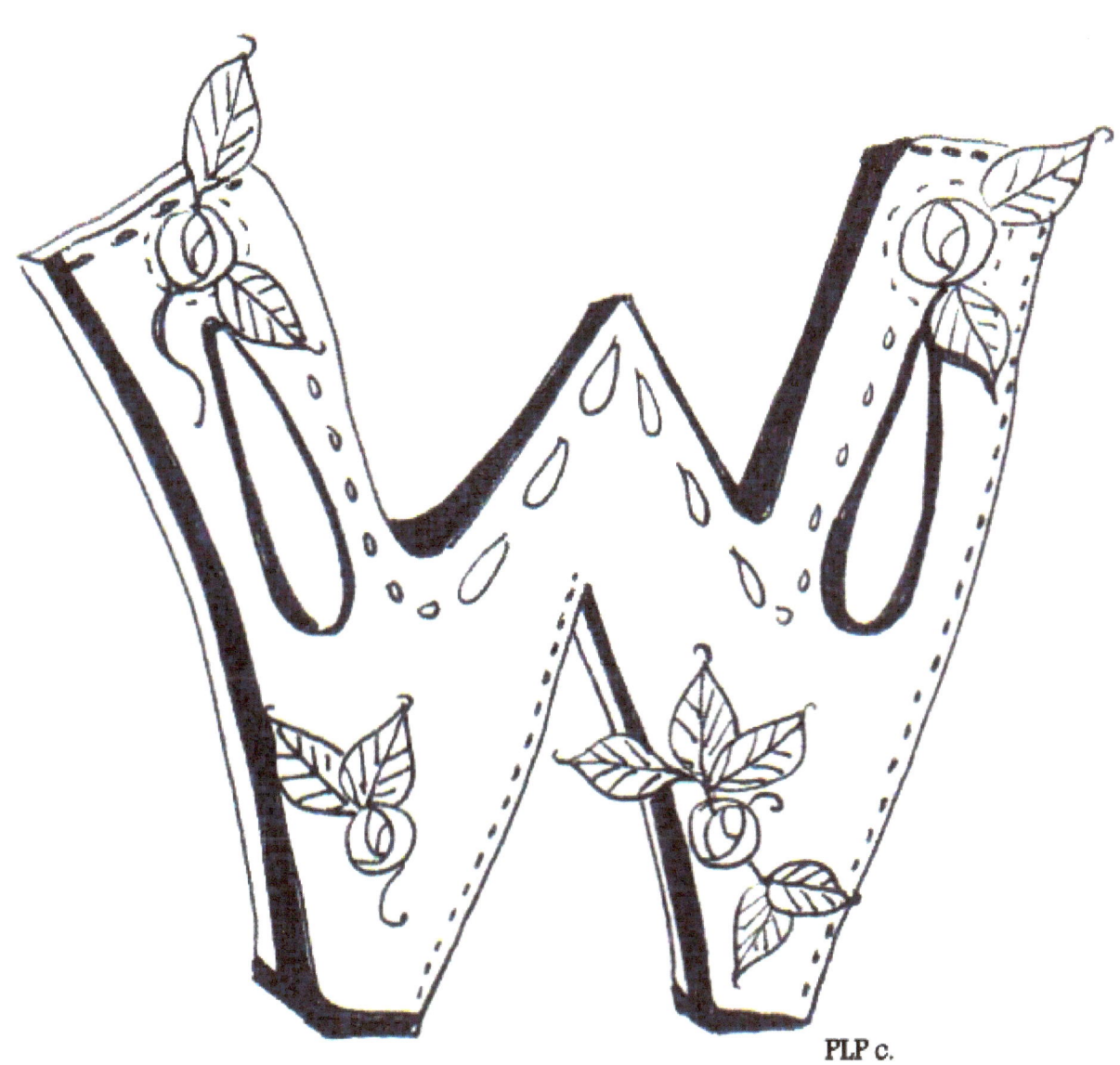

PLP c.

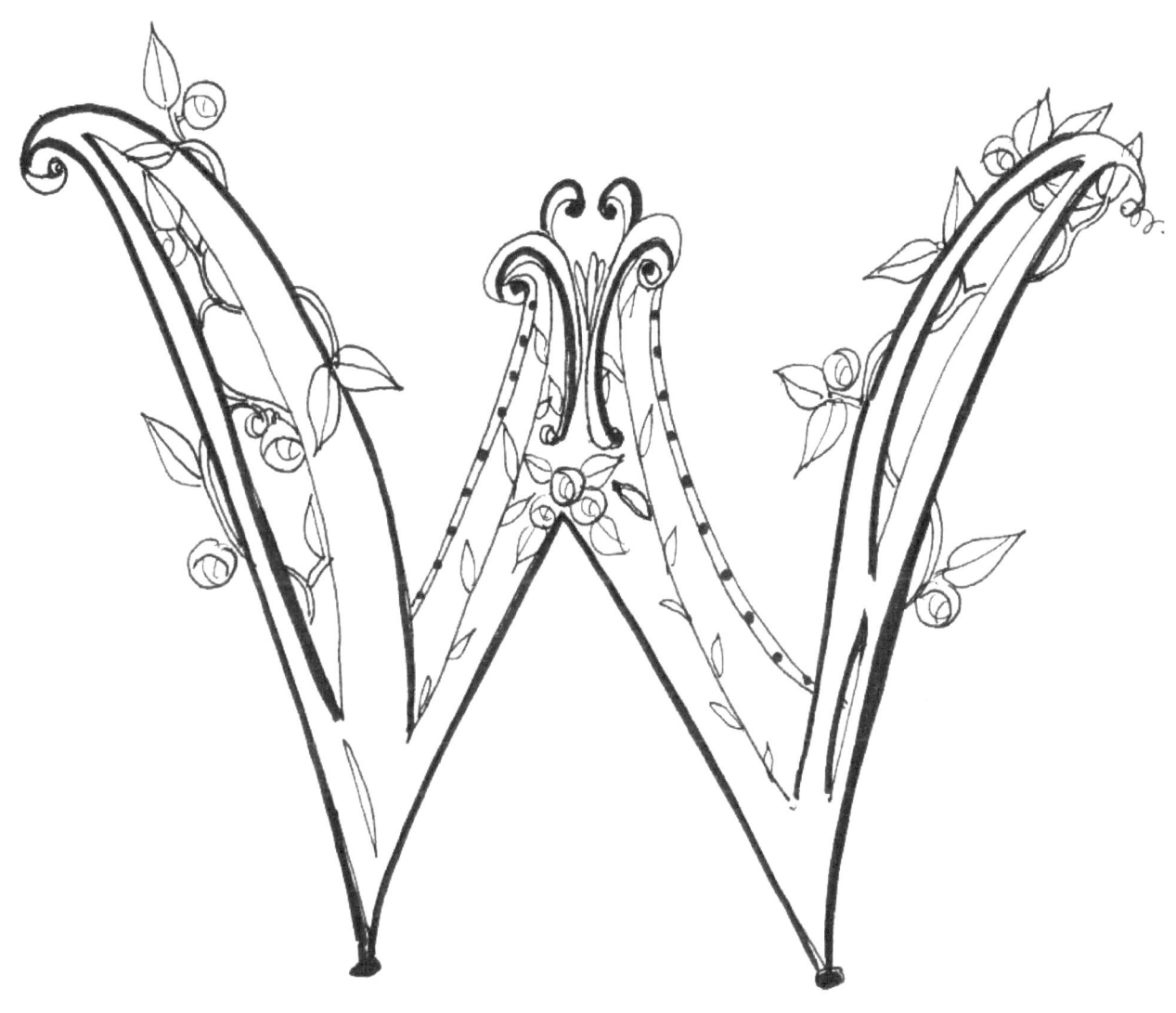

PLP c.

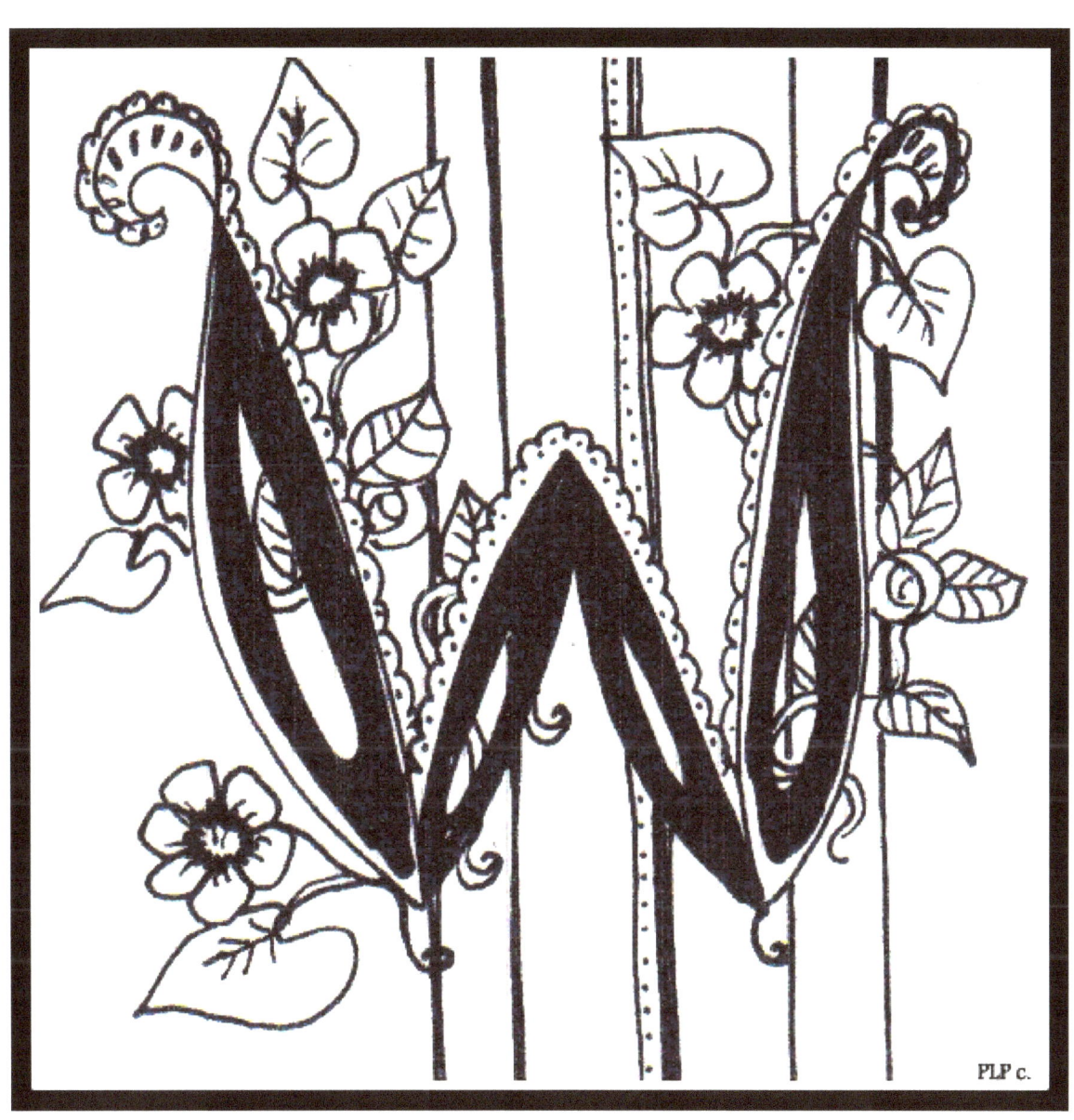

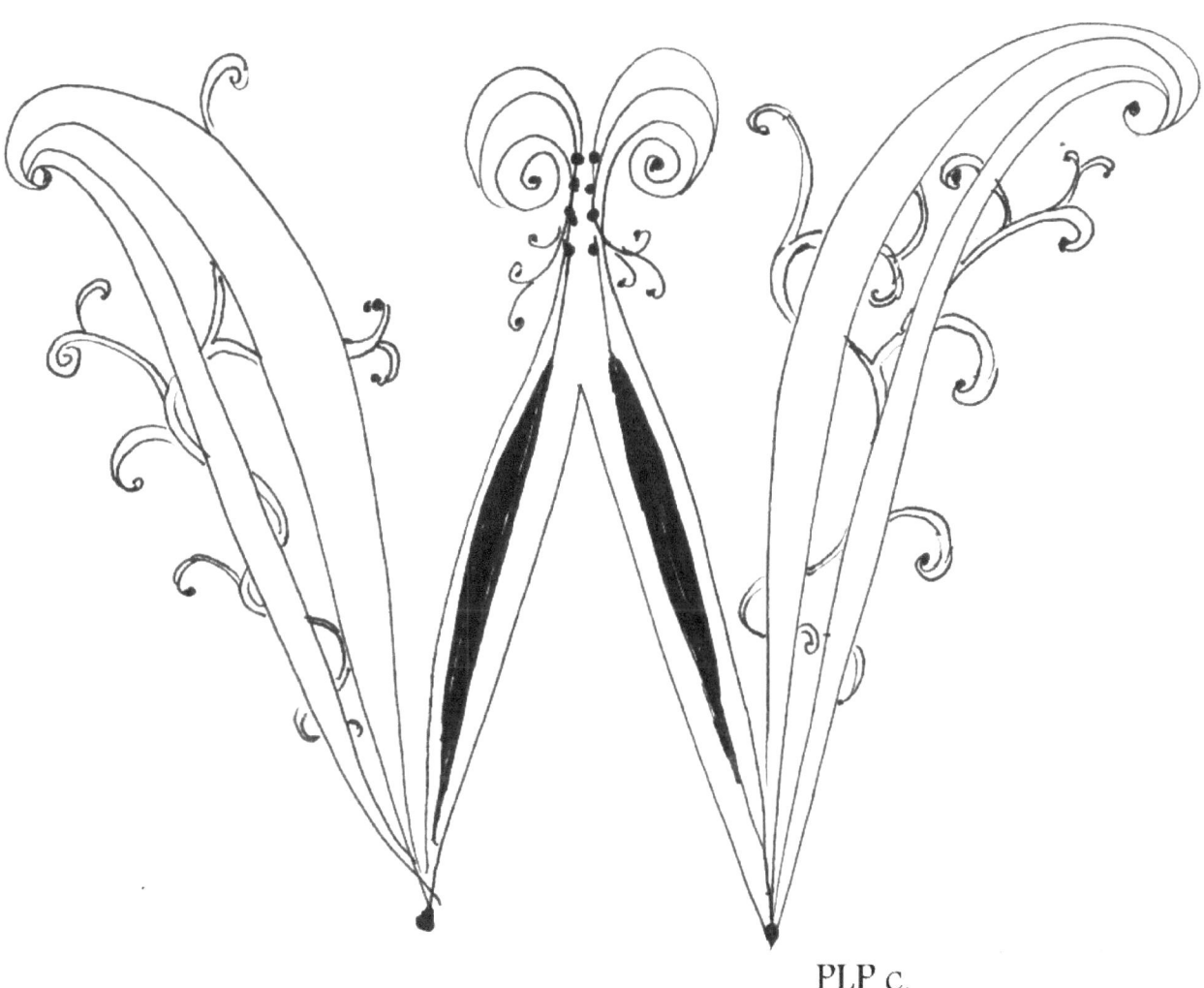

PLP c.

51

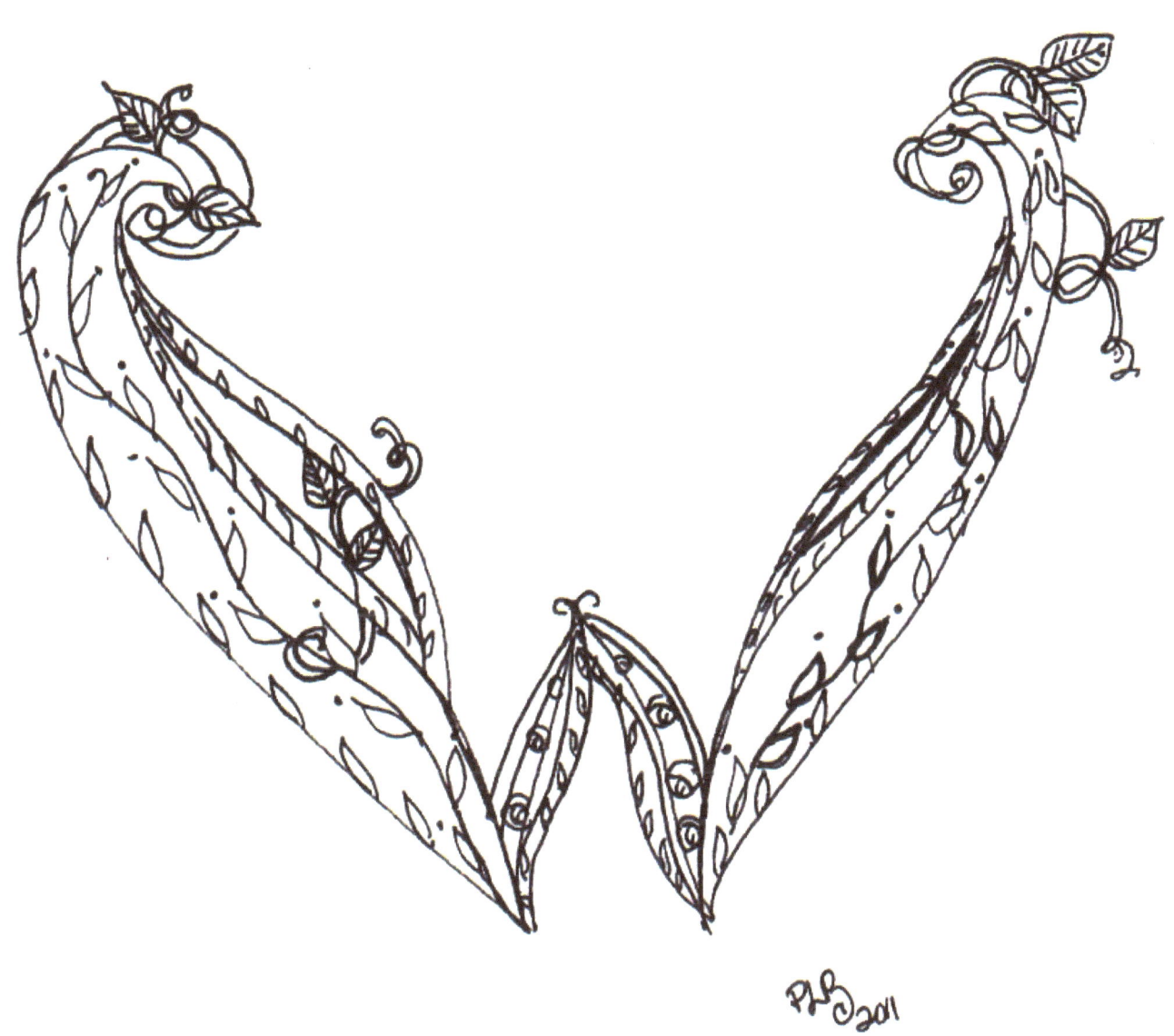

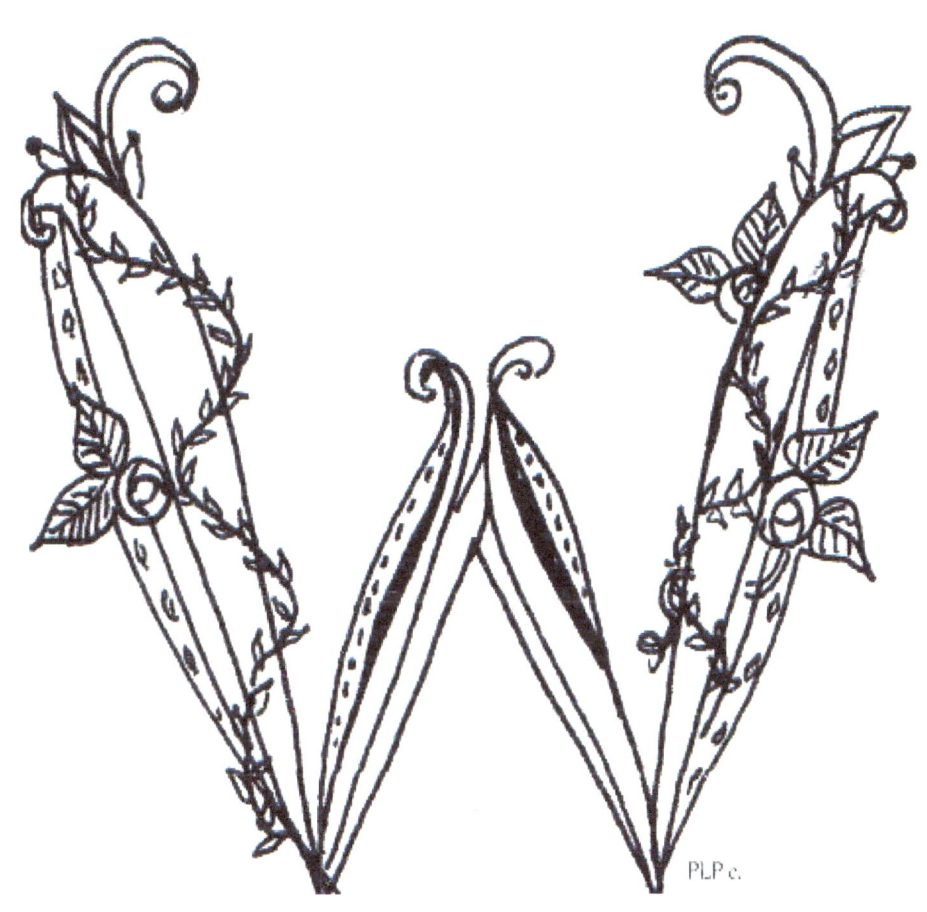

PLP c.

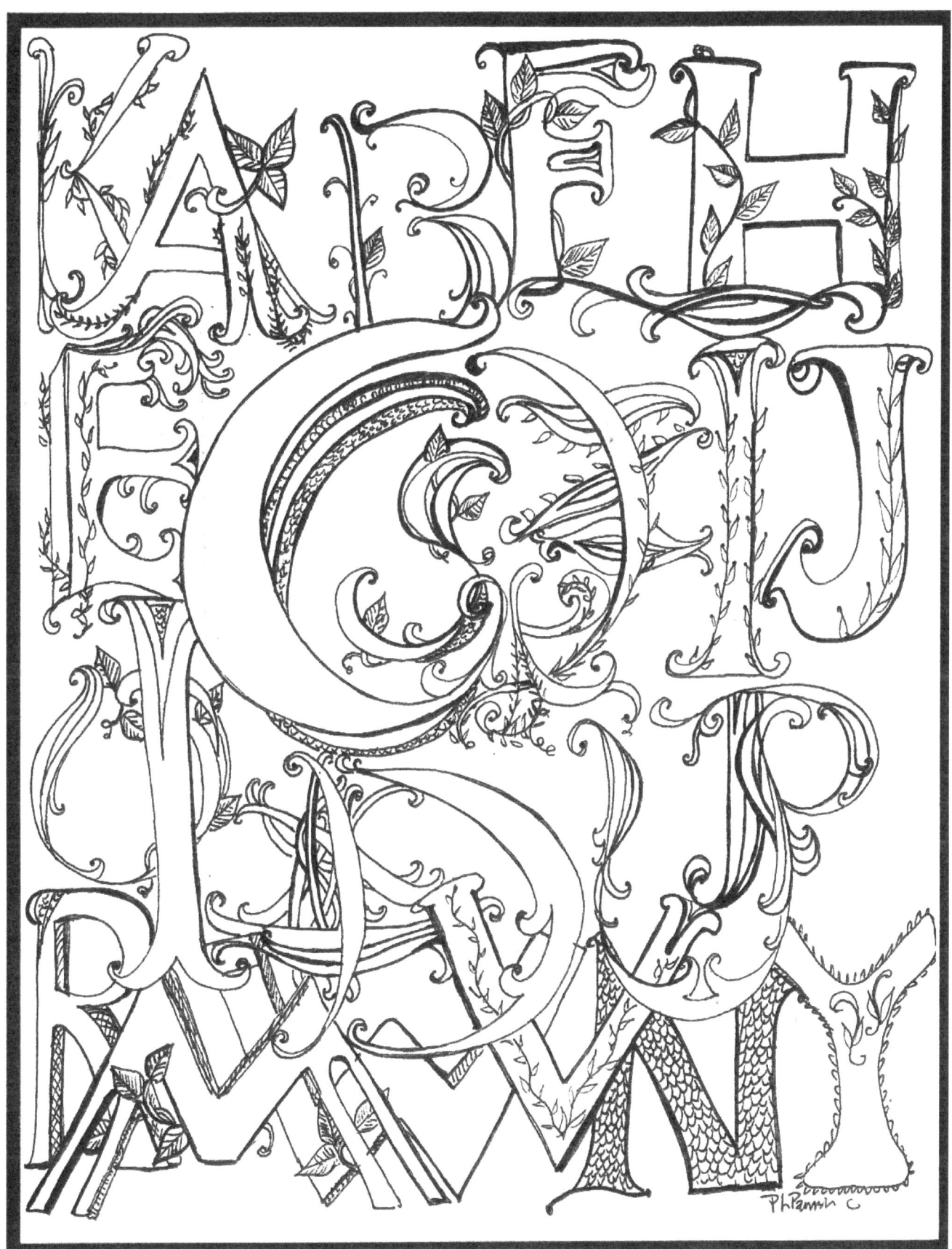

Can you find Letter W in these pictures?

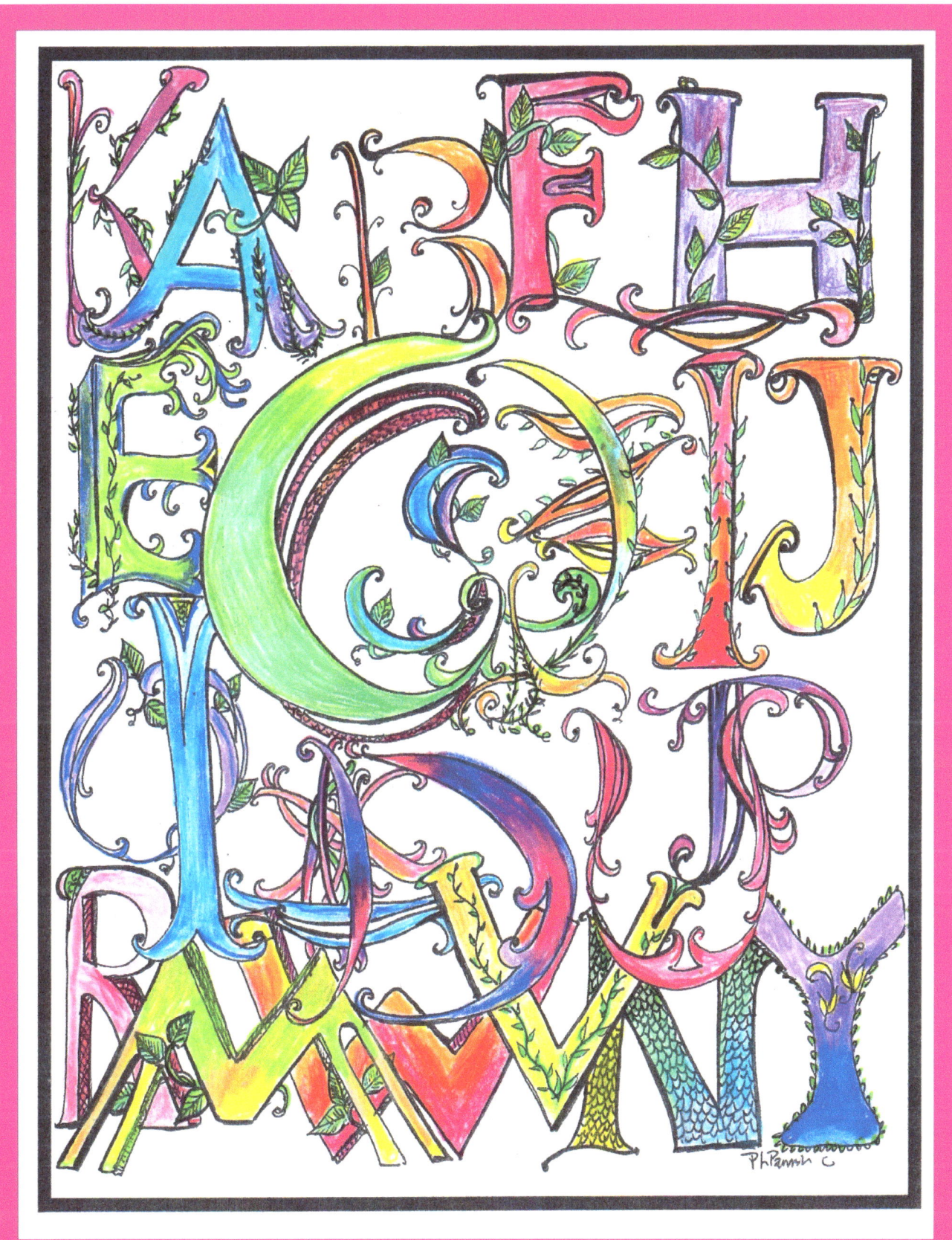

Watch for the other Letter Books By Peggy Louise Parrish.

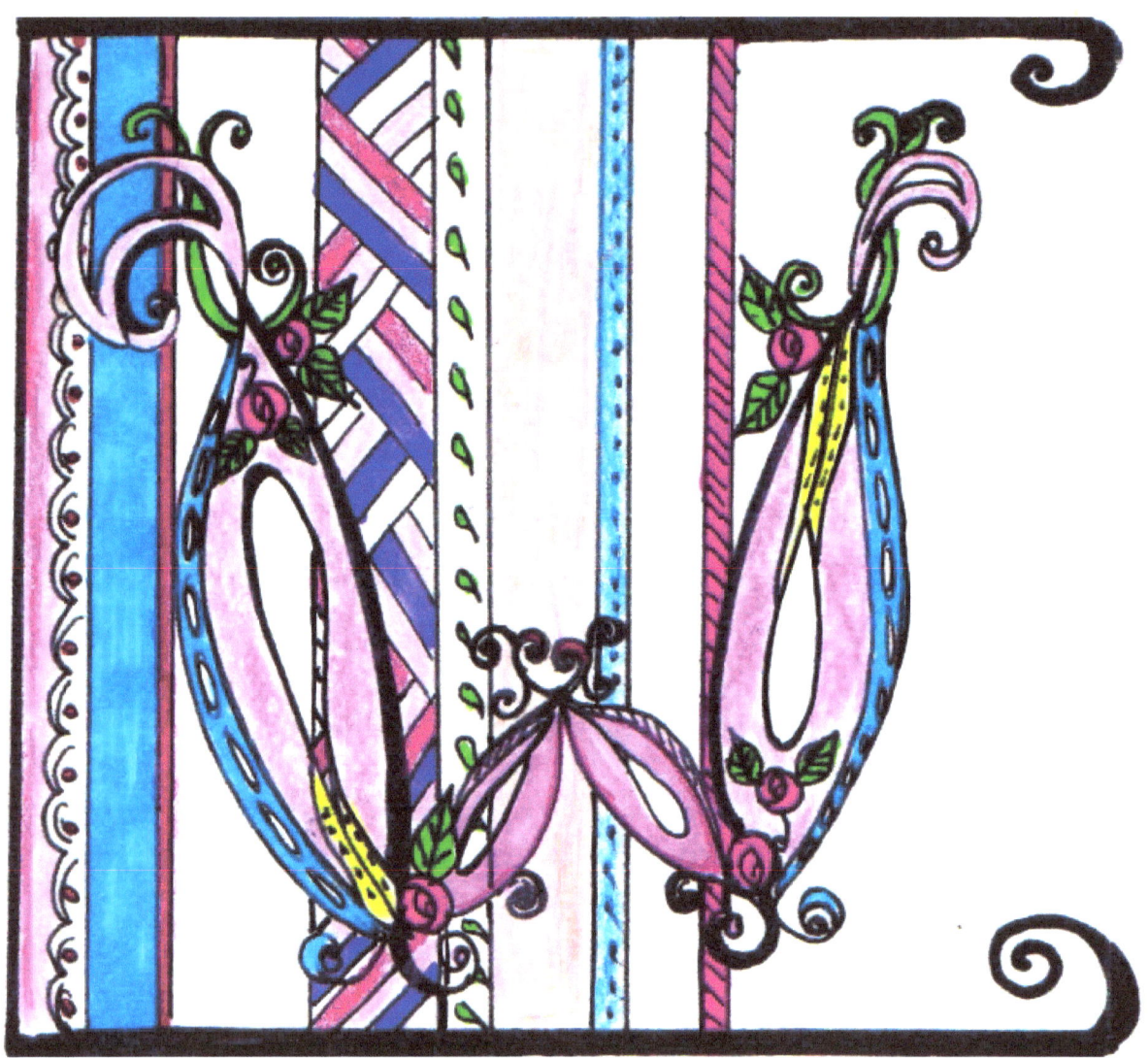

Letter Wonders (PLP)

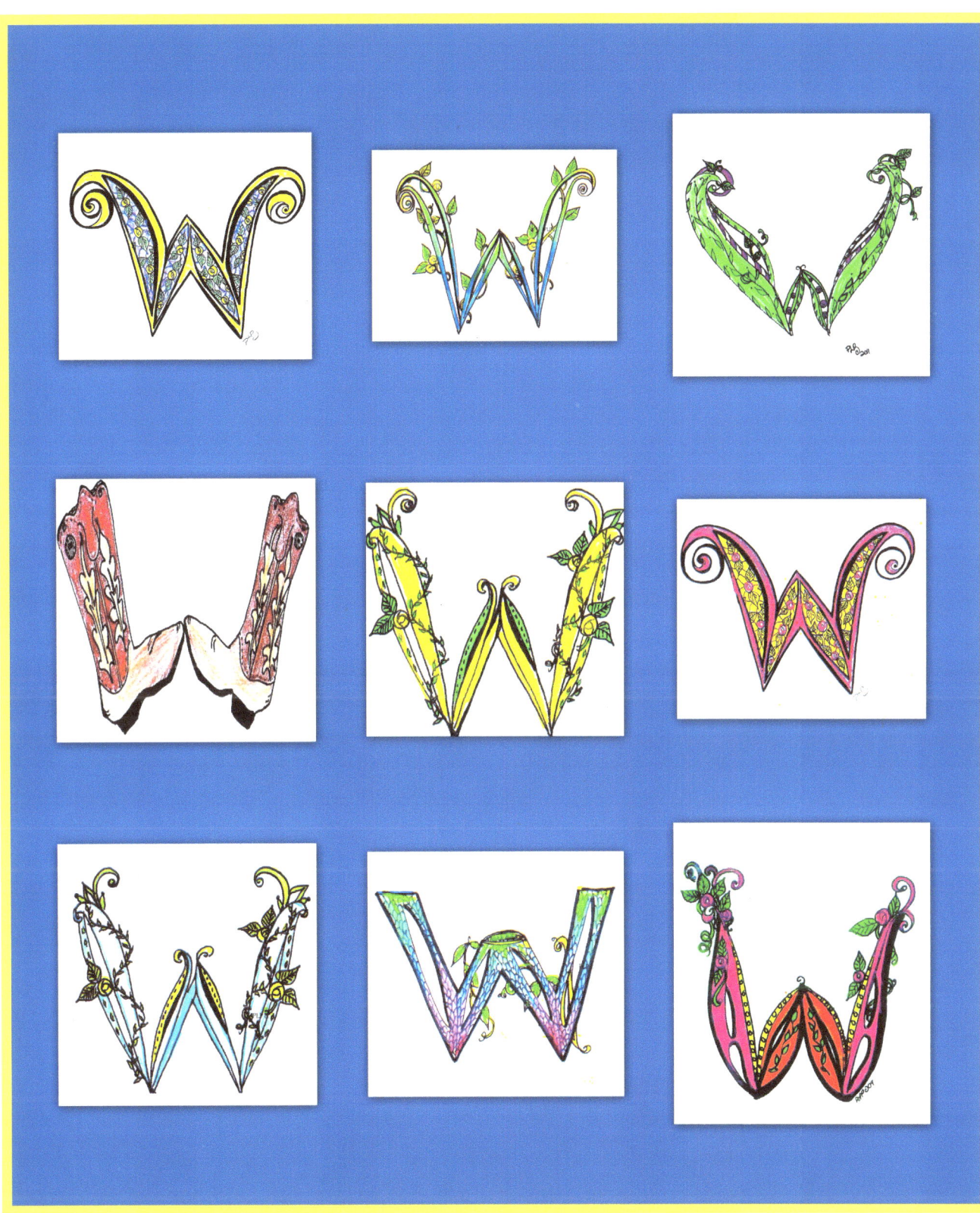

www.ingramcontent.com/pod-product-compliance
Lightning Source LLC
Chambersburg PA
CBHW051048180526
45172CB00002B/552